Student **1B** Book

Apple Pie

Delta's Beginning ESL Program

Sadae Iwataki, Editor

Jean Owensby
Constance Turner
Greta Kojima
Joanne Abing
Jayme Adelson–Goldstein

REVISED EDITION

© 1993 by Delta Systems Co., Inc.
Revised Edition 1995

ISBN 0-937354-57-0

Production Staff:	Geoff Hill
	Diane Bergeron
	Linda Bruell
	Jeannie Patchin
Cover Design:	Geoff Hill
Illustrations:	Jim Ruskowski
	Donna Lewis
	Laura Heuer

Delta Systems Co., Inc.
1400 Miller Parkway
McHenry, IL 60050 U.S.A.

Apple Pie 1B
Table of Contents

Communication Objectives:
    Identify parts of the body
    Ask and answer questions about ailments
    Express sympathy

Structures:
    Simple present of *have*

Communication Objectives:
    Describe simple medical complaints
    Suggest remedies for simple ailments
    Read a Fahrenheit thermometer

New Structures:
    Yes/No questions with *have*
    Short answers *Yes, I do/No, I don't*

Communication Objectives:
    Make medical appointments
    Answer questions about health insurance
    Interpret health insurance card

New Structures:
    Contrast of *Is it . . . ?/Yes, it is* and
                Do you . . . ?/Yes, I do

Unit Nine

Aches, Pains, and Doctors

What's the Matter?

Objectives: In this lesson you will learn to ask and answer questions about what's wrong and express sympathy.

✔ Review: Meeting New Friends

Walk around the classroom and introduce yourself to three students.

S1: Hi! I'm _____.

S2: Hello. My name's _____.

Introduce this new friend to another student.

S: Ivan, this is my friend, Sonia.

Ivan: I'm happy to meet you, Sonia.

Sonia: Pleased to meet you, Ivan.

Something New: Ailments
Listen and Look

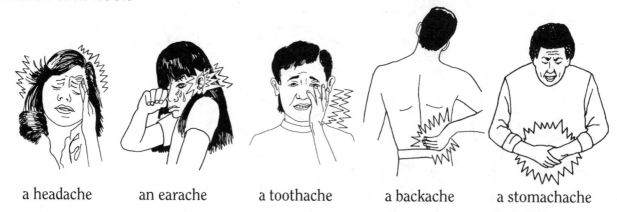

a headache   an earache   a toothache   a backache   a stomachache

Let's Talk: What's the Matter?

Sara: Hi, May. How are you?

May: Not very well, Sara.

Sara: What's the matter?

May: I have a headache.

Sara: Oh, that's too bad.

☛ Practice: "I have a headache"

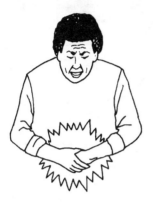

1. S1: What's the matter, Angelo?
   S2: I have a stomachache.

2. S1: What's the matter, Chris?
   S2: I have an earache.

☛ Practice: "That's too bad"

3. S1: What's the matter, Sergio?
   S2: I have a toothache.
   S1: That's too bad.

4. S1: What's the matter, Maria?
   S2: I have a backache.
   S1: That's too bad.

Something New: I Have a Sore Arm

Draw a line from the word to the part of the body.

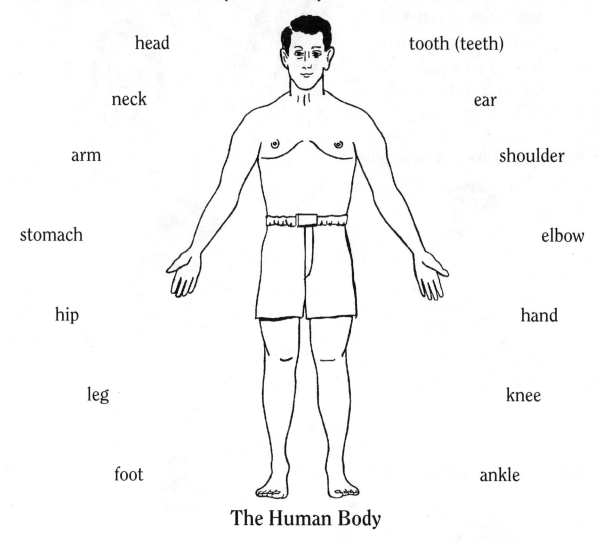

head

neck

arm

stomach

hip

leg

foot

tooth (teeth)

ear

shoulder

elbow

hand

knee

ankle

The Human Body

I have a sore shoulder.

    a sore neck
    a sore arm
    a sore elbow
    a sore hip
    a sore leg
    a sore knee
    a sore ankle
    a sore foot

I have a backache.

    an earache
    a toothache
    a headache
    a stomachache

■ Interaction: I Have a Backache

1. One partner act out (show) an ailment.
2. Ask and answer the question, *"What's the matter?"*
3. Express sympathy. Say, *"That's too bad."*

★ Something Extra: Expressing Sympathy

You can say: "That's too bad."

"I'm sorry to hear that."

☛ Practice: "I'm sorry to hear that"

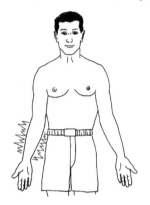

1. S1: What's the matter?
   S2: I have a sore arm.
   S1: That's too bad.

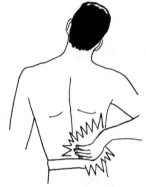

2. S1: What's the matter?
   S2: I have a backache.
   S1: I'm sorry to hear that.

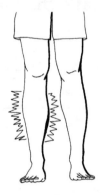

3. S1: - - - - - - - - - - - - - - - - - - ?
   S2: - - - - - - - - - - - - - - - - - .
   S1: - - - - - - - - - - - - - - - - - .

4. S1: - - - - - - - - - - - - - - - - - - ?
   S2: - - - - - - - - - - - - - - - - - .
   S1: - - - - - - - - - - - - - - - - - .

★ Something Extra: Pronunciation

The sound in "ache" is a long sound. It is pronounced /ey/.
Practice with the class and with a partner.

Say: ache   I have a headache.

            ache   I have a toothache.

            ache   I have a backache.

            ache   I have a stomachache.

            ache   I have an earache.

■ Interaction: How Are You?

1. Walk around the classroom.
2. Ask four students, "How are you?"
3. Write their answers.

   Example A: How are you, Mrs. Baker?

                       I'm fine.

   Example B: How are you, Wanda?

                       Not very well.

                       What's the matter?

                       I have a sore knee.

	Name	How are you?	What's the matter?
A.	Mrs. Baker	fine	
B.	Wanda	not very well	sore knee

Reading: I Feel Terrible

I'm at home today. I'm not at work. I have a headache. I have a backache and sore shoulders. I have sore arms and legs. I'm in bed. I feel terrible.

Discussion

1. How do you feel today?
2. What's the matter?
3. Are you at work?
4. Where are you?

 **Writing**

1. What's the matter?

    I have _____ .

2. What's the matter?

    I _____

    _____

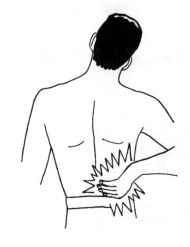

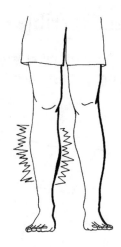

3. _____ ?

I have a backache.

4. What's the matter?

_____ sore leg.

☞ Practice Activity: Simon says

1. Stand up and follow the teacher's directions **only** when the teacher says, "Simon says . . ."

   Teacher: Simon says, "Touch your knee."

   Students: (Touch your knee.)

   Teacher: Touch your arm.

   Students: (Don't move.)

2. **Remember!** If the teacher doesn't say "Simon says," **don't move**.

A. Listen to the directions and write the number under the correct picture.

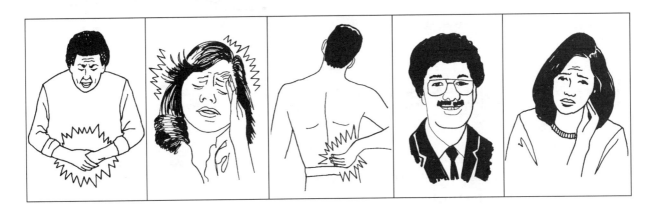

B. Partner 1 read the directions. Partner 2 follow the directions. Then change roles.

1. Touch your nose.
2. Pat your head.
3. Put your elbows on the table.

4. Look at your foot.
5. Point to your stomach.
6. Rub your stomach and pat your head.

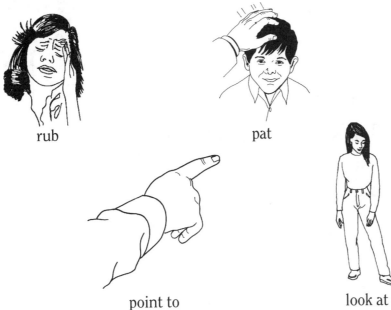

rub   pat   touch

point to   look at

Now Partner 1 give new directions. Partner 2 follow the directions.
Then change roles again.

Do You Have a Fever?

Objectives: In this lesson you will learn to tell a doctor about simple ailments, and to read a U.S. thermometer.

✔ Review: What's the Matter?

Use the pictures to ask and answer questions.

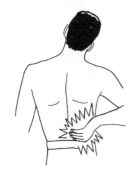   

Something New: What's Your Temperature?
Listen and Look

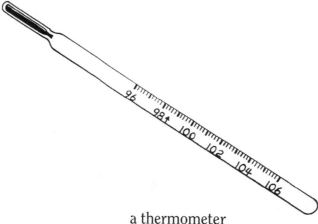

a thermometer

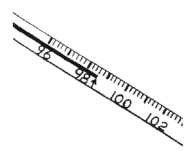

My temperature is normal. It's 98.6.

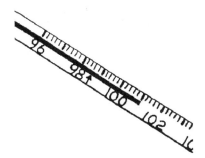

My temperature is 101. I have a fever.

☛ **Practice: "My temperature's 102"**

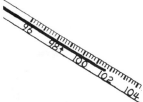

1. S1: Do you have a fever?
   S2: Yes, I do. My temperature's almost 102.

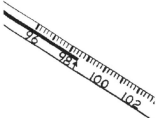

2. S1: Do you have a fever?
   S2: No, I don't. My temperature's normal.

3. S1: Do you have a stomachache?
   S2: Yes, I do.

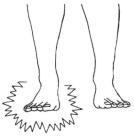

4. S1: Do you have a sore foot?
   S2: Yes, I do.

5. S1: Do you have a sore arm?
   S2: No, I don't. I have a sore shoulder.

6. S1: Do you have a sore ankle?
   S2: No, I don't. I have a sore knee.

Something New: Symptoms

I think I have the flu.

a headache

a sore body

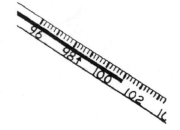

a fever

I think I have a cold.

a cough

a runny nose

a sore throat

Let's Talk: Do You Have a Fever?

Susie: Hello, Dr. Chu. This is Susie Vo. I think I have the flu.

Dr. Chu: Do you have a fever, Miss Vo?

Susie: Yes, I do.

Dr. Chu: What's your temperature?

Susie: It's a hundred.

Dr. Chu: Take an aspirin and stay in bed.

★ Something Extra: Suggesting Remedies

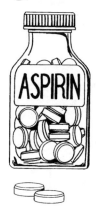

aspirin

Medicine for the flu
for a fever
for a headache

cold medicine

Medicine for a cold
for a cough
for a runny nose

■ Interaction: Home Remedies

1. What home remedy do you take for a cold?
    for a backache?
    for a headache?

2. Tell your group you have an ailment.
    What remedy do they suggest?

    Example: S1: What's the matter?

    S2: I have a cough.

    S3: Drink hot lemonade and honey.

Reading: Calling in Sick

Tranh has a bad cold. He is calling the manager at the restaurant.

Tranh:	Hello, Mrs. Serra. This is Tranh. I'm sick today. I have a bad cold.
Mrs. Serra:	Stay home. Drink a lot of liquids.
Tranh:	Liquids?
Mrs. Serra:	Water, fruit juice, soup. . .
Tranh:	Oh, okay.
Mrs. Serra:	Take care, Tranh.
Tranh:	Thank you.

Questions

1.	Tranh is sick.	Yes	No	I don't know.
2.	Tranh has a fever.	Yes	No	I don't know.
3.	Mrs. Serra has a cold.	Yes	No	I don't know.
4.	Water is a liquid.	Yes	No	I don't know.

✍ **Writing**

Mrs. Serra: _____ the matter, Tranh?

Tranh: I have a bad cold. I have a cough, _____ , and

_____ .

Mrs. Serra: I'm _____ to hear that. _____ in bed and

_____ a lot of liquids.

Tranh: Okay.

Mrs. Serra: _____ care, Tranh.

A. Listen to the nurse and write the correct temperature.

1. _____   4. _____

2. _____   5. _____

3. _____   6. _____

B. Talk about the picture.

1. Are Mrs. Lee's children at school?
2. Where are they?
3. What's the matter with the children?
4. Is it lunch time?
5. What's for lunch?

C. These people have problems. Write the remedy.

Go to bed.
Don't smoke.

Drink hot tea with lemon and honey.
Drink a little soda.

Call the dentist.
Take an aspirin.

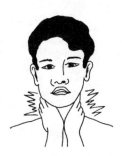

1. _Drink hot tea with lemon and honey._

2. _____

3. _____

4. _____

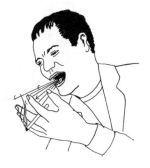

5. _____

6. _____

D. Tic Tac Toe: "What's the matter?"

Choose a square for your team.

Answer the question correctly and your team gets the square.

Get 3 squares in a row, your team is the winner!!

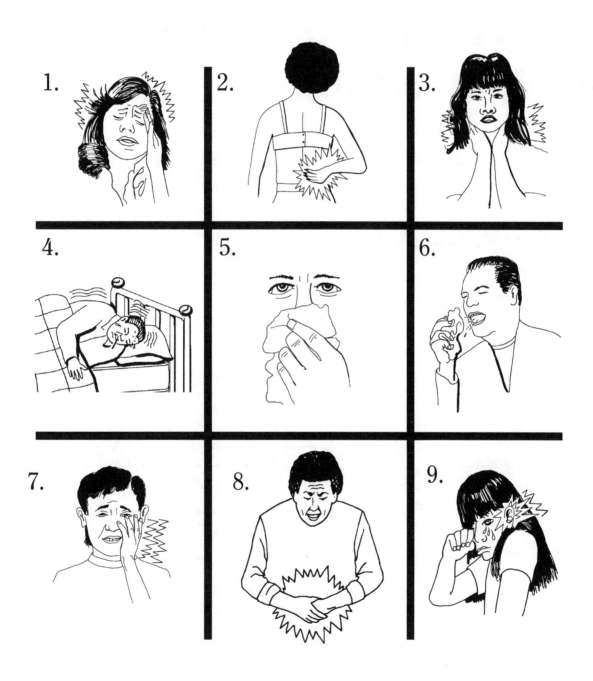

I Have an Appointment with Dr. Chu

Objectives: In this lesson you will learn to read an appointment card, go to the doctor's office, and answer questions about health insurance.

✔ Review: Parts of the Body

1. Draw a person on the chalkboard.
2. Write the parts of the body.
3. Talk about ailments and remedies.

Something New: An Appointment Card and a Health Insurance Card

1. What's this?
2. Who is the doctor? Who is the patient?
3. When is the appointment?
4. What time is the appointment?

DR. DAVID CHU, M.D.
APPOINTMENT

PATIENT: *Sara Gomez*

DATE: *Wednesday, February 21*

TIME: *10:00 A.m.*

An Appointment Card

1. What's this?
2. Who is the card for?
3. What is the name of the insurance plan?

HEALTH ASSOCIATION PROGRAM

SARA GOMEZ
0001-6662

A Health Insurance Card

Discussion

1. Do you have an appointment with a doctor or a dentist?
2. When is your appointment? What time? Do you have an appointment card?
4. Do you have a health insurance card? Show it to the class.

Let's Talk: I Have an Appointment

Sara:	I have a 10 o'clock appointment with Dr. Chu. My name is Sara Gomez.
Receptionist:	Good morning, Mrs. Gomez. Is this your first visit here?
Sara:	Yes, it is.
Receptionist:	Do you have insurance?
Sara:	Yes, I do. Here is my card.
Receptionist:	Thank you. Please take a seat.

☛ **Practice: "I have a 3:30 appointment"**

1. S1: I have a 3:30 appointment
        with Dr. Hall.
   S2: Please take a seat.

2. S1: I have a 9:45 appointment
        with Dr. Morrison.
   S2: Please take a seat.

3. S1: Do you have an
        appointment?
   S2: Yes, I do.

4. S1: Do you have an
        appointment?
   S2: Yes, I do. I have an 8:15
        appointment with Dr. Chu.

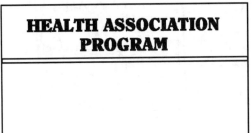

5. S1: Do you have insurance?
   S2: Yes, I do.

6. S1: Do you have insurance?
   S2: No, I don't.

Reading: Late for an Appointment

Tom is late. His doctor's appointment is at 10:00. It is ten now, but he is still in the parking lot.

The doctor's office is on the fourth floor. The elevator is slow. It's always slow when a person is in a hurry!

Tom is in the doctor's office. "I'm sorry I'm late," he says. "That's all right. The doctor is late, too," says the receptionist.

Discussion

1. Why is Tom worried? What's the matter?
2. Why does the receptionist say, "It's all right?"
3. Are you ever late for appointments? How do you feel when you are late?

■ **Interaction:** Your Next Appointment

1. One partner is a patient and one partner is a receptionist.
2. Talk about the next appointment and fill out the appointment card.

    Example: Receptionist: Your next appointment is Wednesday, May 22.

    Is 9:00 okay?

    Patient: That's fine.

3. Then change roles and practice again.

✍ Writing

Dr. Block, M.D.

APPOINTMENT

DATE: *Wed. 10/5*

TIME: *2:45*

1. Receptionist: Do you have an appointment?

   Patient: _____ . _____ a 2:45

   appointment _____ Dr. Block.

Dr. Luis Flores, M.D.

APPOINTMENT

DATE: *Thursday, 3/12*

TIME: *11:15 a.m.*

2. Receptionist: _____ ?

   Patient: Yes, _____ . I _____

   _____ .

**HEALTH ASSOCIATION
PROGRAM**

~signature~

1 2 3 4 5 6 7 8 9

3. Receptionist: Is this your first visit?

   Patient: Yes, _____ .

   Receptionist: _____ you _____ insurance?

   Patient: Yes, _____ .

Lesson 27 Activity Pages

A. Write the appointment times.

1. _____10:45_____   4. _____   7. _____

2. _____   5. _____   8. _____

3. _____   6. _____   9. _____

B. Talk about the appointment cards.

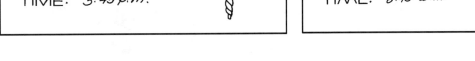

DR. JONES, M.D.
APPOINTMENT

PATIENT: *Jae Kim*

DATE: *July 10*

TIME: *3:45 p.m.*

DR. KIM, D.D.S.
APPOINTMENT

PATIENT: *Linda Jones*

DATE: *June 10*

TIME: *8:45 a.m.*

C. Write the answer.

1. Who is Jae Kim's doctor? _____

2. When is Mrs. Kim's appointment? _____

3. Is Linda's appointment on June 10 or July 10? _____

4. What time is Linda's appointment? _____

D. BINGO!!

Ask and answer *"Do you have..."* questions.

When the answer is yes, write the student's name on the line.

Get three names in a row and you have BINGO!

Unit Nine Evaluation

I. Listening Comprehension

Listen and circle the correct answer, A or B.

1.

   A    B

2.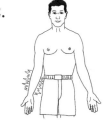

   A    B

3.

   A 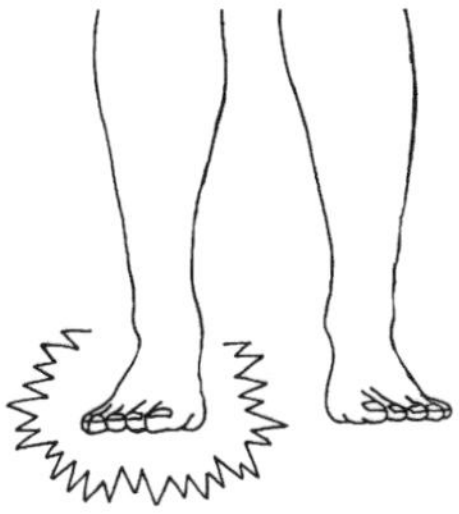   B

4.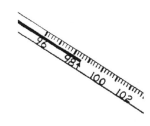

   A 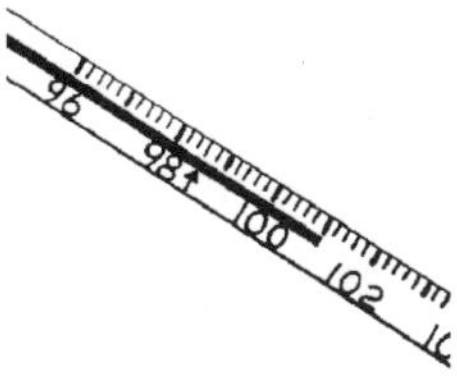   B

5.

   A. Yes, I do.   B. No, I don't.

6.

Dr. Grey M.D. Next Appointment Day: Tuesday Time: 10:30	Dr. Grey M.D. Next Appointment Day: Thursday Time: 2:30
A	B

7.

Dr. Grey M.D. Next Appointment Day: Tuesday Time: 10:30	Dr. Grey M.D. Next Appointment Day: Thursday Time: 2:30
A	B

8.

   A   B

II. Reading

Circle the correct answer.

1. I have _____ .

   toothache   sore arm   a fever

2. _____ you have a sore knee?

   How   Do   Are

3. Is your temperature normal?

   Yes, _____ .

   it's   it is   it isn't

4. _____ the matter?

   What   What's   How

5. Drink _____ and go to bed.

   sore throat   aspirin   fluids

III. Writing

Choose the correct word and write it on the line.

1. Mrs. Baker: Dr. Chu, this _____ Mrs. Baker.

   I think I have the_____ .

2. Dr. Chu: Do _____ have a fever?

3. Mrs. Baker: _____ , I do.

4. Dr. Chu: What's your _____ ?

5. Mrs. Baker: It's 101.

6. Dr. Chu: _____ an aspirin and

   _____ in bed.

flu
is
stay
Take
temperature
Yes
you

Unit Ten
Family Ties

HOME SWEET HOME

Ana's Our First Child

Objectives: In this lesson you will learn to discuss relatives and families.

✔ Review: Calling in Sick

Act out an ailment or hold up a picture and practice.

> S1: I'm not very well today.
>
> S2: What's the matter?
>
> S1: My whole body aches.
>
> S2: Take an aspirin and go to bed.

Something New: Family Tree

Listen and Look

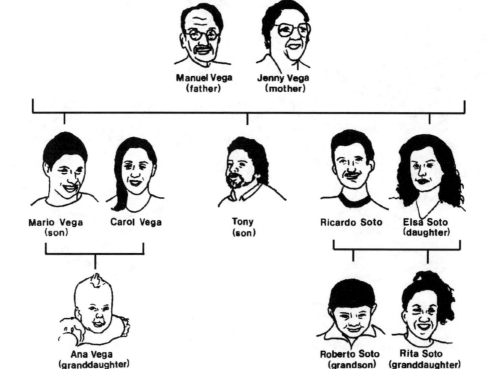

The Vega Family Tree

Manuel Vega (father) Jenny Vega (mother)

Mario Vega (son) Carol Vega Tony (son) Ricardo Soto Elsa Soto (daughter)

Ana Vega (granddaughter) Roberto Soto (grandson) Rita Soto (granddaughter)

Delta's Apple Pie, Book 1B

☞ Practice Activity: The Vega family

Look at the family tree. Ask and answer the questions in your group.

1. How many children do Manuel and Jenny have?
2. Are the children all married?
3. Who is Carol?
4. Who is Ricardo?
5. Is anyone single?
6. How many brothers and sisters does Tony have?

Let's Talk: Ana's Our First Child

Mario Vega is showing pictures of his new baby to May Lei.

Mario: This is Ana. She's three months old today.

May: She's beautiful! How many children do you have now?

Mario: Just one. Ana's our first child. Do you have any children?

May: No, I don't. I'm single and I don't have any children.

☛ Practice: "Do you have any children?"

1. S1: Do you have any children?
   S2: Yes, I do. I have three.

2. S1: Do you have any brothers or sisters?

   S2: Yes, I do. I have a brother and two sisters.

3. S1: Does she have any children?

   S2: No, she doesn't. She's single.

4. S1: Does Bill have a family here?

   S2: No, he doesn't. His family is in Canada.

5. S1: How many children do you have?

   S2: I have two sons and two daughters.

6. S1: How many children does he have?

   S2: He doesn't have any. He's single.

■ Interaction: Do You Have a Large Family?

1. With a partner, ask and answer questions about your families:

   Do you have a large family?

   How many children do you have? Are they boys or girls?

   Do you have any brothers or sisters?

   How many brothers/sisters do you have?

2. One student ask about other people in the class.

   Does he/she have a family?

   How many children does he/she have?

★ Something Extra: Relationships

Look at the family tree on page 28 again. There are many relationships in a family. Manuel and Jenny Vega are the father and mother of Mario, Tony, and Elsa, but that's not all.

Who are Manuel and Jenny Vega?

father / mother	of Mario, Tony, Elsa
father–in–law / mother–in–law	of Carol, Ricardo
grandfather / grandmother	of Ana, Roberto, Rita

Manuel and Jenny Vega

And what about Mario?

son	of Manuel and Jenny
brother	of Tony and Elsa
husband	of Carol
brother–in–law	of Ricardo
uncle	of Roberto and Rita

Mario

And Ana?

daughter	of Mario and Carol
granddaughter	of Manuel and Jenny
niece	of Tony, Elsa and Ricardo
cousin	of Roberto and Rita

Ana

☛ Practice Activity: Relationships

Write as many relationships as you can for:

Tony _____

Carol _____

Ricardo _____

Elsa _____

Rita _____

Roberto _____

Reading: The Single Parent

There are many families in the United States with single parents. Rosa is a single mother. Her daughter, Linda, is 14 years old. Her husband died in an automobile accident two years ago. Rosa has a bad leg from that accident, but she works all day in an office. Linda is a big help to her mother around the house.

Discussion

1. What is a single parent?
2. What happened to Rosa's husband?
3. What is Rosa's problem?
4. How does Linda help her mother?
5. What do you think are some of the problems of single parents?

✍ Writing

Look at the family tree on page 28 and fill in the blanks.

1. Manuel Vega is Mario's _____.

   Carol's _____.

   Ana's _____.

2. Carol Vega is Mario's _____.

   Jenny's _____.

   Elsa's _____.

   Rita's _____.

☛ Practice Activity: Who's this?

1. Draw your family tree in the space below.
2. Then with a partner, ask and answer questions about your family trees.

My Family Tree

Lesson 28 Activity Pages

A. *Listen and write the missing names on Milly's family tree.*

Names: Bob, Frank, Gary, Hannah, Karl, Sara, Sue

B. Write questions or answers about Milly's family.

1. Is Milly married or single?

   Milly is _____.

2. _____ children _____ Milly _____?

   She has two.

3. Is Ruth Milly's _____?

   Yes, she is.

4. Does Ruth have any children?

   Yes, _____ a son. His name is Gary.

5. Who is Martha?

   She is Milly's _____.

6. Does Sue have any children?

   _____.

How Many Bedrooms Are There in Your Apartment?

Objectives: In this lesson you will talk about rooms in an apartment or house.

✔ Review: A Family Tree

1. Look at your teacher's family tree.
2. Ask questions about your teacher's family.

Something New: Rooms in an Apartment
Listen and Look

These are rooms in an apartment or house.

a living room

a dining room

a bedroom

a kitchen

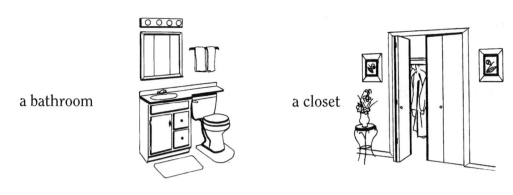

a bathroom   a closet

☛ Practice: "It's a living room"

1. S1: What's this?
   S2: It's a living room.

2. S1: Is this a kitchen or a dining room?
   S2: It's a dining room.

Something New: Mario and Carol's Apartment

Mario and Carol Vega live in a one–bedroom apartment.

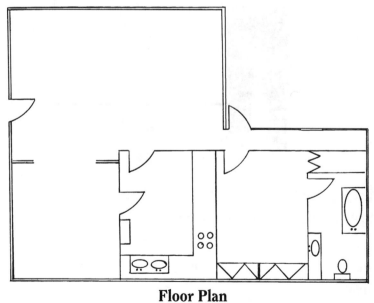

Floor Plan

☞ Practice: "Is there a kitchen in the apartment?"

Answer these questions about Mario and Carol's apartment:

1. Is there a kitchen in the apartment? ___*Yes, there is.*___

2. Is there a bathroom in the apartment? _____

3. Are there two bedrooms in the apartment? _____

4. Is there a dining room in the apartment? _____

5. Are there two closets in the apartment? _____

Let's Talk: How Many Bedrooms Are There?

Mario wants a larger apartment. He is talking to a friend at work.

Mario: My apartment is very small. I want a large apartment.

Luz: How many bedrooms are there in your apartment?

Mario: There's only one. And we have a new baby.

Luz: There's a vacancy in my building. Come and see the manager.

Mario: Thanks, Luz.

Delta's Apple Pie, Book 1B

☛ Practice: "Is your apartment small?"

1. S1: Is your apartment small?
    S2: Yes, it is.

2. S1: Is your bedroom small?
    S2: No, it isn't. It's large.

3. S1: Is there a bedroom in your apartment?
    S2: Yes, there is.

4. S1: Are there many windows?
    S2: Yes, there are.

5. S1: How many bathrooms are there in the apartment?
    S2: There's just one.
    S1: Is it a large bathroom?
    S2: Yes, it is.

6. S1: How many closets are there in the apartment?
    S2: There are two.
    S1: Are they large closets?
    S2: No, they aren't. They're very small.

■ Interaction: A Floor Plan

1. On a piece of paper, draw a floor plan of your partner's apartment or house.
    Ask questions to help you draw the floor plan.

    Examples: Is there a dining room in your apartment/house?

    How many bedrooms are there?

    How many closets are there? Where are they?

2. Show the floor plan to the class and talk about your partner's apartment or house.

Reading: An Apartment or a House

Nina is looking for a house. She doesn't want another apartment. She wants a yard for her children and a garden for vegetables. There is a big garden in Nina's home in Mexico. She wants to find a house with a yard.

Discussion

1. Does Nina live in an apartment or a house?
2. Why does she want a house?
3. Do you live in an apartment or a house?
4. Do you have a yard?
5. Do you have a garden? What kind of plants do you have?
6. Do you have plants in your house?
7. Tell about your home in your native country.

✍ **Writing:** My Dream Home

Make a floor plan of an apartment or house that you want. Name the rooms.

A. *Listen and label the picture. Write the names of the rooms on the floor plan.*

bedroom	bathroom	kitchen	living room	dining room

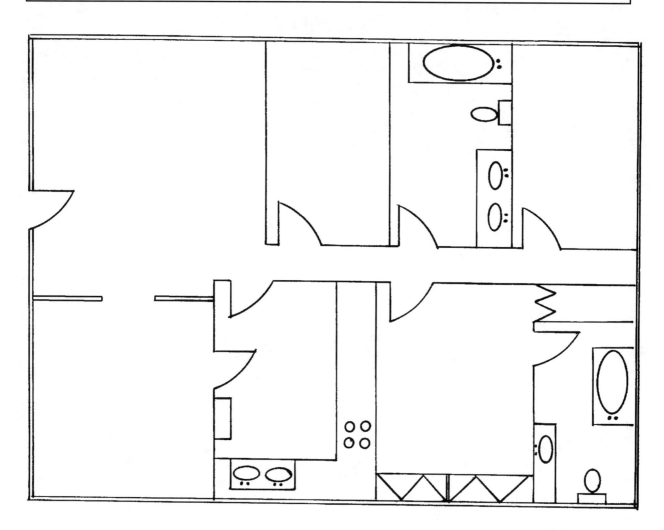

B. Read and circle the correct word. Copy the correct sentence.

1. There are three (bedroom/bedrooms) in Rosa's apartment.

   _____

2. There are (two/three) bathrooms in her apartment.

   _____

3. There (is/are) two closets in her bedroom.

   _____

4. There (is/are) a kitchen in her apartment.

   _____

5. (Is/Are) there a dining room in her apartment?

   _____

6. Yes, (there/they) is. It's a small dining room.

   _____

7. Now write one question and answer about Rosa's apartment.

   _____

   _____

   _____

C. Information Gap: How many bedrooms are there?

Sit with a partner. Partner 1 looks at page 44 and Partner 2 looks at page 45. Ask and answer questions to fill in the chart.

Partner 1

Examples: Partner 1: How many bedrooms are there in Apartment A?

Partner 2: There are 3. How many bathrooms are there in Apartment B?

Partner 1: Just one.

	Apartment A	Apartment B	Apartment C
Bedrooms			
Bathrooms	2	1	1
Closets		3	6
Rooms		5	

Partner 2

Examples: Partner 1: How many bedrooms are there in Apartment A?

Partner 2: There are 3. How many bathrooms are there in Apartment B?

Partner 1: Just one.

	Apartment A	Apartment B	Apartment C
Bedrooms	3	2	2
Bathrooms			
Closets	4		
Rooms	8		5

Is There a Bus Stop Nearby?

Objectives: In this lesson you will learn to ask about an apartment for rent.

✔ Review: A Floor Plan

1. Draw a floor plan of your house or apartment on the board.
2. Ask and answer questions about it.

Examples: Is there a dining room in the apartment?

Are there closets in the apartment?

How many bedrooms are there in the apartment? Etc.

Something New: New Apartment
Listen and Look

Do you need a new apartment?

What kind of apartment do you want?

a furnished apartment

an unfurnished apartment

How do you find a new apartment?

1. Ask friends and relatives.
2. Look in the newspapers.
3. Look for signs.

APT. FOR RENT

1—2 Br.
Furn.—Unfurn.
See Mgr.

VACANCY

Apartment
1Br. 1 Ba.
Call 555-5460

Abbreviations

Br.—Bedroom	Apt.—Apartment	Furn.—Furnished
Mgr.—Manager	Ba.—Bathroom	Unfurn.—Unfurnished

Let's Talk: Is There a Bus Stop Nearby?

Mario and Carol are at Luz's building. They are talking to the manager about an apartment.

Mario:	I want a two–bedroom apartment. Do you have a vacancy?
Manager:	Yes, I do.
Mario:	How much is the rent?
Manager:	It's $650 a month.
Carol:	Is there a bus stop nearby?
Manager:	Yes, there is. There's one on the corner.

☛ **Practice: "I want a two–bedroom apartment"**

FOR RENT
2 Br.
Furn. — Unfurn.
See Mgr.

No Vacancy

1. S1: What do you want?
   S2: I want a two–bedroom apartment.

2. S1: Do you have an apartment for rent?
   S2: No, I don't.

☞ **Practice: "How much is the rent?"**

```
┌─────────────────────┐     ┌─────────────────────┐
│     Apartment       │     │     Apartment       │
│     for Rent        │     │     for Rent        │
│       $475          │     │       $600          │
└─────────────────────┘     └─────────────────────┘
```

3. S1: How much is the rent?   4. S1: How much is the rent?
    S2: It's _____ .   S2: It's _____ .

☞ **Practice: "Is there a school nearby?"**

5. S1: Is there a school nearby?   6. S1: Are there stores nearby?
    S2: Yes, there is.   S2: Yes, there are.

☞ **Practice Activity: Apartment for rent**

Make a FOR RENT sign for your
house or apartment.

How many bedrooms are there?

How many bathrooms?

Is it furnished?

What's the rent?

```
┌──────────────────────────────────┐
│                                  │
│        _____          │
│                                  │
│     _____      │
│                                  │
│     _____      │
│                                  │
│     _____      │
│                                  │
└──────────────────────────────────┘
```

■ Interaction: Calling the Manager

1. Practice calling about an apartment.
2. Think of questions you can ask.
3. Practice with a partner.

APTS.

CALL
555-5498

Example: S1: Hello?

S2: Hello. Do you have a two–bedroom apartment for rent?

S1: Yes, I do.

S2: Is there a parking space?

S1: Yes, there is.

S2: How much is the rent? Etc.

Reading: A Three–story Building

There are 12 apartments in Anita's building. It has three floors. It is a three–story building. Anita's apartment is on the third floor. There is no elevator in the building. Anita wants an apartment on the first floor.

Discussion

1. Does Anita live in a large apartment building?
2. How many apartments are there in her building?
3. What is a three–story building?
4. Why does Anita want to move?
5. Do you live in an apartment building? Talk about your building. Is it large? Where is your apartment?

✍ Writing

A. Complete the questions and answers about this apartment.

1. _____ there an apartment _____ rent?

2. Yes, _____ is.

3. How _____ is the rent?

4. It's _____ a month.

5. How _____ bedrooms

   _____ there in the apartment?

6. There _____ one.

> VACANCY
> 1 Br. Apt.
> $475

B. Write three questions about this sign and answer them.

1. _____

   _____

   _____?

   _____

   _____

   _____.

2. _____

   _____

   _____?

   _____

   _____.

3. _____

   _____

   _____?

   _____

   _____.

> APTS.
> 1–2 Br.
> $400–$600

Lesson 30 Activity Page

A. Listen and check the information you hear.

	House	Apartment	1 bdrm.	2 bdrm.	3 bdrm.	1 ba.	2 ba.	nr. bus	nr. school
1. Ky									
2. Carlos									
3. Magda									
4. Felix									

B. Match the people with the homes they want. Look at the chart above and write the correct name under the sign.

```
FOR RENT
Clean 3 bdrm., 2 ba.
nr. schools, shopping
Unfurn. $850
```

_____

```
FOR SALE
by Owner
3 bdrm., 2 ba.
Lg. yd., nr. mall
$240,000
```

_____

```
FOR RENT
2 bdrm., 2 ba.
Nice yd., Quiet
Unfurn. $650
Call eves. 889-0980
```

_____

```
VACANCY
Nice 1 br., nr. univ.
Unfurn., 1st and last
$400
See mgr.
```

_____

Unit Ten Evaluation

I. Listening Comprehension

Listen and circle the correct answer, A or B.

1.

   A   B

2.

   A   B

     Manuel and Jenny Vega

Mario and Carol Vega   Tony Vega   Ricardo and Elsa Soto

3.   A. Yes   B. No   4.   A. Yes   B. No

5.

   A   B

6.

   A. Yes, there is.   B. Yes, it is.

7.   A. Yes, there are.

   B. No, there aren't.

   HOUSE
   FOR RENT
   3 Br.
   2 Ba.

8.

   A. Yes, she is.

   B. Yes, she does.

II. Reading

Circle the correct answers.

1. I don't have _____ children.

     no   not   any

2. How many children _____ you have?

     are   do   not

3. There _____ a mall nearby.

     have   is   are

4. Are there many closets?

     Yes, _____.

     they are   there is   there are

III. Writing

Choose the correct words.

1. Yee and Lin _____ three children.

FOR RENT
3 Bdrms.
Unfurn.
$500

2. They want a _____ apartment.

3. The rent is $500 _____ month.

4. There _____ three bedrooms in the apartment.

| a |
| are |
| have |
| large |
| no |

5. There is _____ furniture in the apartment.

Unit Eleven

Food and Fun

We Love Mandy's Southern Fried Chicken

Objectives: In this lesson you will learn to order chicken in a fast–food restaurant.

✔ **Review:** Your Home

1. In small groups, ask and answer questions about your homes.

   Examples: Do you live in an apartment?
   How many apartments are there in the building?

   Is there a laundry room in your apartment building?

   a swimming pool?

   a play area for children?

   What are the apartment rules about pets?

   about parking?

   about visitors?

2. Tell the class about your group.

Something New: Parts of a Chicken
Listen and Look

A Chicken

Pieces of Chicken

Dark Meat

drumstick

thigh

White Meat

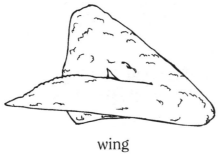

wing

breast

☛ **Practice: "I like white meat"**

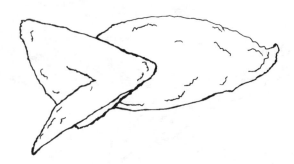

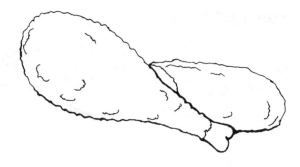

1. S1: Do you like chicken?
   S2: Yes, I do.
   S1: Do you like white or dark meat?
   S2: I like white meat.

2. S1: Does your brother like chicken?
   S2: Yes, he does.
   S1: Does he like white or dark meat?
   S2: He likes dark meat.

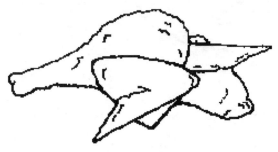

3. S1: Do your children like chicken?
   S2: Yes, they do. They love it!
   S1: Do they like white or dark meat?
   S2: (They like) both.

4. S1: Does your wife like chicken?
   S2: Yes, she does. She really likes it.
   S1: What part does she like?
   S2: She likes wings.

5. S1: Do you like chicken?
   S2: Yes, I do.
   S1: What's your favorite piece?
   S2: I like drumsticks.

6. S1: What's your favorite part
       of the chicken?
   S2: I like - - - - - - - - - - - - - .

Let's Talk: At Mandy's

Mandy's Southern Fried Chicken

MEALS

3 pieces   8 pieces   12 pieces
5 pieces   10 pieces   15 pieces

includes coleslaw, corn on the cob, biscuits, gravy

CHICKEN BY THE PIECE

box — 8 pieces   bucket — 10 pieces
large bucket — 12 pieces   barrel — 15 pieces

All White or Dark Meat — 15 cents extra, each piece

Mandy: May I help you?

Mrs. Kim: Yes, please. I'd like a
           barrel of chicken. And I
           want four extra pieces
           of dark meat, please.

Mandy: All right, that's 15
           pieces, and four extra
           pieces of dark meat.
           Do you want drumsticks
           or thighs?

Mrs. Kim: Drumsticks, please.

Mandy: Anything else?

Mrs. Kim: No, that's all.

☛ Practice: "I'd like three pieces"

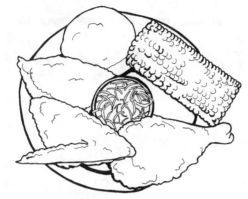

1. S1: May I help you?
   S2: Yes. I'd like the 3–piece meal, please.
   S1: Okay. A 3–piece meal.

2. S1: May I help you?
   S2: I'd like two pieces of white meat.
   S1: That's two pieces of white meat.

3. S1: Do you want some chicken?
   S2: Yes, I do. I want two
   pieces of dark meat.

4. S1: Does your son want a drumstick?
   S2: Yes, he does.

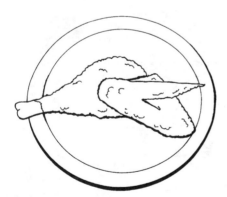

5. S1: What do you want?
   S2: I want a wing and a drumstick.

6. S1: What does Lucy want?
   S2: She wants some white meat.

■ Interaction: Taking an Order

1. Look at the Mandy's menu on page 59.
2. Partner 1 order chicken from Mandy's. Partner 2 take the order.
3. Change roles: Partner 2 order and Partner 1 take the order.

☛ Practice Activity: Planning a party

Plan a party for yourself and four classmates. You need fried chicken from Mandy's for the party. Write what kind of chicken you like, and then as four friends.

1. Do you like white meat or dark meat?
2. What's your favorite piece?
3. Are you a big eater?

Name	Dark	White	Favorite Piece	Big Eater?

How many pieces do you need for the party?

Do you need white meat, or dark meat, or both?

Reading: Chicken Is Healthy

People today are careful about health. They are careful about food. They don't eat much red meat. They eat a lot of chicken. Chicken is good for people. It is healthy. It is good for the heart.

Discussion

1. Is chicken good for people? Why?
2. Do you eat a lot of chicken?
3. What part of the chicken do you like?
4. Do you like fried chicken?
5. What kind of chicken dishes do you like?

✎ Writing

1. Does Joe like dark or white meat?

   _____ dark meat.

2. What _____ he

   _____ today?

   He wants drumsticks.

3. Do you like dark or white meat?

   _____

   _____ .

4. What do you want today?

   _____

   _____ .

Lesson 31 Activity Page

A. Listen and make a check under the order for each family.

✓ ORDER FORM • Mandy's Southern Fried Chicken • ORDER FORM ✓							
	barrel 15 pieces	lg. bucket 12 pieces	bucket 10 pieces	box 8 pieces	coleslaw 1 pint	potatoes 1 pint	lunch special 3 pieces/coleslaw
1.							
2.							
3.							
4.							
5.							

B. Ask and answer the questions with your partner. Circle the answers.

	YOU	YOUR PARTNER
Do you like white meat or dark meat?	white meat	white meat
	dark meat	dark meat
Do you like coleslaw or salad?	coleslaw	coleslaw
	salad	salad
Do you like potatoes or rice?	potatoes	potatoes
	rice	rice
Do you like soda or milk?	soda	soda
	milk	milk

Unit Eleven

Lesson 32

He Likes Italian Food

Objectives: In this lesson you will talk about types of food people like and don't like.

✔ Review: Pieces of Chicken

Name the pieces of chicken. Are they white or dark meat?

1. It's a _____*wing*_____ .

    _____*white meat*_____

2. They're _____ .

    _____

3. _____ .

    _____

4. _____

    _____

Delta's Apple Pie, Book 1B

Something New: International Foods
Listen and Look

Italian food	**Chinese food**	**Japanese food**
pizza spaghetti	chow mein lemon chicken	sushi teriyaki chicken

Mexican food	**American food**	**Armenian food**
a tostada a taco	fried chicken a hamburger	shish kebab pita bread

☞ Practice: "Mary likes American food"

1. I like Mexican food.
   I'm hungry.
   I want a tostada today.

2. Mary likes American food.
   She's hungry. She wants
   fried chicken.

3. Tom likes Chinese food. He's hungry. He wants chow mein today.

4. Mr. and Mrs. Nelson like Italian food. They're hungry. They want spaghetti.

5. Jim likes Japanese food.

He's hungry. He wants teriyaki chicken.

6. We like - - - - - - - - - - - - - - - .

We're hungry. We want

- .

Discussion

What kinds of food do you like?

What do you want today?

What's your favorite kind of food?

Are you hungry?

Let's Talk: What Do You Want to Eat?

Tom and Sam are ready for lunch.

Tom: Are you hungry, Sam?

Sam: Yes, I am.

Tom: Do you like Mexican food?

Sam: Oh, yes. It's my favorite food.

Tom: What do you want to eat?

Sam: I want tacos.

☛ Practice: "Are you hungry?"

1. S1: Are you hungry?
   S2: Yes, I am.
   S1: Do you want a hamburger?
   S2: Yes, I do.

2. S1: Is your son hungry?
   S2: Yes, he is.
   S1: Does he want some fried chicken?
   S2: Yes, he does.

3. S1: Do you like Chinese food?
   S2: Yes, I do.
   S1: Do you want some chow mein?
   S2: Not today. Maybe some
       lemon chicken.

4. S1: Does your daughter like
       Italian food?
   S2: Yes, she does.
   S1: Does she want some pizza?
   S2: Oh, yes! She does!

★ Something Extra: I'm Thirsty
Listen and Look

1. I'm thirsty.
   I want some water.

2. Sue is thirsty.
   She wants a soda.

3. Sam is thirsty, too.
   He wants some iced tea.

Do you like iced tea? Coffee? Milk?

What do you want today?

What's your favorite drink?

Reading: International Foods

We live in a world of change. People like to eat foods from all over the world. People in Los Angeles eat Korean food. People in Mexico City eat Italian food. People in London eat Chinese food. People in Moscow eat hamburgers from McDonald's!

Discussion

1. Do you try foods from different countries?
2. What kinds of food do you like?
3. Are you hungry right now? What do you want to eat?

✍ Writing

1. Are you hungry?

   _____ .

   Do you want a hamburger?

   Yes, _____ .

2. Is Sue thirsty?

   Yes, _____ .

   What does she want to drink?

   _____ some water.

3. _____ you and Ben hungry?

Yes, _____ .

What _____

want to eat?

_____ Chinese food.

4. _____ Tom hungry?

Yes, he is.

_____

_____ to eat?

He wants spaghetti.

✎✎ More Writing

Write about yourself. What kinds of food do you like? What's your favorite kind of food?
What do you want to eat today?

_____

_____

_____

_____

_____

_____

_____

Lesson 32 Activity Pages

A. Listen to Mark talk about his friends.

✔ Make a check under the foods they like to eat.

✘ Make an x under the foods they don't like.

	Italian	Japanese	American
Lola			
Kumiko			
Carla			
Ben			

B. Look at the grid and answer the questions.

1. What kind of food does Lola like?

   _____

2. What kind of food does Kumiko like?

   _____

3. What's the matter with Carla?

   _____

4. Does Ben like to eat hamburgers and hot dogs?

   _____

Delta's Apple Pie, Book 1B

C. Guess! What kind of food is it?

Work with two other people.

1. Write your guesses.
2. Compare your guesses with the other two people.

_____ 1. Greek	a. piroshki
_____ 2. French	b. tandoori chicken
_____ 3. German	c. baklava
_____ 4. Russian	d. patipat
_____ 5. Korean	e. bratwurst
_____ 6. Thai	f. crepes suzette
_____ 7. East Indian	g. bul gogi

D. Group Grid

Work with a group. Ask each person in the group about the kind of food they like. Write **yes** or **no** on the grid. Talk about your answers.

Do you like _____ food?

NAME	Italian	Chinese	Mexican	Armenian	French
Maria	*yes*	*no*	*yes*	*no*	*yes*

E. Plan a party.

Look at the grid on page 71 and plan a party with your group.

Plan the time and the date.

Plan the food and the drinks.

Write your information on the invitation.

Please come

to our _____ *party!*
      (What kind of food?)

On _____
      (What date?)

At _____
      (What time?)

At _____
      (Where?)

F. Write a story about your party.

We _____ to have a party on _____ at

_____ . We all like _____ food

and we want to serve _____ and

_____ . We want to drink _____ or

_____ . We _____ to have a good

time, listen to music, dance and _____ .

G. Draw a picture of your party. Show it to your partner and talk about it.

Lesson 33

I Like American Movies

Objectives: In this lesson you will learn to talk about different kinds of movies. You will also learn to make suggestions.

✔ Review: Food from Different Countries

1. Talk about food from your country.

    Examples: What's a special food for holidays?

                         What's your favorite food from your country?

2. Tell the class about the other students in your group and their favorite foods.

Something New: Kinds of Movies
Look and Listen

I like action movies.

Sue and Michi like cartoons.

Jim is crazy about westerns.

Henry likes horror movies.

My wife and I love
science fiction movies.

My mother loves comedies.

Let's Talk: Let's Rent a Movie

Mila: Do you like movies?

Hank: I'm crazy about them.

Mila: What's your favorite
kind of movie?

Hank: I like science fiction.

Mila: There's a video store
down the street. Let's go there
and rent a space movie.

Hank: Great idea. I want to see
"Space Wars" again!

☛ Practice: "Do you like horror movies?"

1. S1: Do you like horror movies?
   S2: No, I don't.

2. S1: Does Joe like westerns?
   S2: Yes, he does.

3. S1: Let's rent a comedy.
   S2: Okay, let's do it.

4. S1: Let's rewind the tape.
   S2: Okay. Go ahead.

5. S1: Let's see the movie again.
   S2: Good idea!

6. S1: Let's return the video.
   S2: Okay. Let's go.

■ Interaction: Movies

What kind of movies do you like?

What kind of movies do your friends like?

Ask four students.

Name	Like movies?	Favorite kind?

★ Something Extra: Making Suggestions

You can use *Let's* to make a suggestion to a friend.
Write your suggestion and your friend's response.

Suggestion	Response
Let's make popcorn.	*Good idea!*
Let's get some chips and soft drinks.	

Reading: A Movie Rating Guide for Parents

What kind of movies are good for children? Is there a guide for parents? Yes, there is. There is a rating guide for movies.

A **"G"** rating means General. It's a family movie.

A **"PG"** rating means Parental Guidance. Parents can decide if they want their children to see the movie. **"PG–13"** suggests parental guidance for children 13 and under.

An **"R"** rating means "Restricted." Children 17 years old and under need to go to the movie with an adult.

An **"X"** rating means the movie is for adults only.

Discussion

1. Review what the ratings mean.
2. Do you look at the rating when you choose a movie?
3. What movies do you choose for your children?

■ Interaction: Movie Ratings

1. With a partner, look at the movie posters on pages 74 and 75.
2. Discuss each movie:

   What kind of movie is it?

   Is it good for children?
3. Give each movie a rating for parents.

✍ Writing

1. Ask your partner what kind of movies and food he/she likes and doesn't like.
2. Write sentences about you and about your partner.

Likes	**Dislikes**

Movies

I like _____

_____ .

My partner likes _____

_____ .

I don't like _____

_____ .

He/She doesn't like _____

_____ .

Food

I like _____

_____ .

My partner likes _____

_____ .

I don't like_____

_____ .

He/She doesn't like _____

_____ .

Lesson 33 Activity Pages

A. Tell the story to your partner.

B. Match the statements to the people in the pictures on page 79.

a. mother   b. father   c. child

_____ 1. This person likes horror movies.

_____ 2. This person likes cartoons.

_____ 3. This person likes romantic movies.

_____ 4. This person likes science fiction movies.

_____ 5. This person doesn't like romantic movies.

_____ 6. This person doesn't like horror movies.

Unit Eleven  Evaluation

I. Listening Comprehension

Listen and circle the correct answer, A or B.

1.

   A   B

2.

   A   B

3.

   A   B

4.

   A   B

5. A. Yes, I am.
   B. Yes, I do.

6. A. Yes, she is.
   B. Yes, she does.

7.

   A. He wants a taco.
   B. I want a taco.

8.

   A. He likes white meat.
   B. Yes, he does.

II. Reading

Circle the correct answer.

1. _____ you like white meat or dark meat?

      Are   Do   Not

2. He _____ to eat spaghetti.

      wants   like   is

3. _____ Sara hungry?

      Is   Does   Have

4. They _____ Chinese food.

      like   are   likes

5. _____ rent a video.

      Have   Let's   Like

6. _____ Bill like horror movies?

      Is   Not   Does

III. Writing

Choose the correct words and write them in the story.

Mr. and Mrs. Kim _____ hungry and thirsty. They _____ American food. Mrs. Kim _____ a hamburger. Mr. Kim _____ want a hamburger. He wants fried chicken. _____ likes dark meat. He wants some thighs and _____.

are
doesn't
drumsticks
He
like
wants

82   Delta's Apple Pie, Book 1B

Unit Twelve

What's Going On?

Lesson 34

You Need a Heavy Jacket

Objectives: In this lesson you will identify and describe some items of clothing and talk about the seasons of the year.

✔ Review: The Movies

1. Name six different kinds of movies. Give an example of each.

2. Discuss movies in your country.
   Did you watch American movies in your country?
   What language did the actors speak?

3. What are your favorite movies?

4. Who are your favorite movie stars?

Something New: Clothing
Listen and Look

Let's look in Tomas and Sara's closet.

a short dress   a long skirt

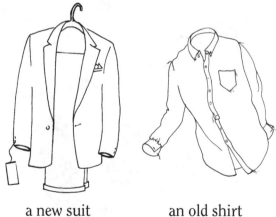

a new suit   an old shirt

a narrow tie   a wide belt   a light coat   a heavy jacket

☛ **Practice: "What's in the closet?"**

1. S1: What's in the closet?
   S2: A light jacket.

2. S1: What's in the closet?
   S2: A short skirt.

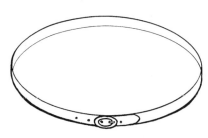
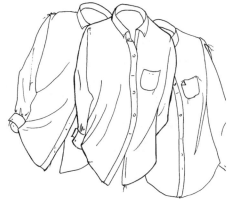

3. S1: Is there a wide belt in Sara's closet?
   S2: No, there isn't. That's a narrow belt.

4. S1: Are there many new shirts in his closet?
   S2: No, there aren't. Those are old shirts.

Something New: Seasons

Spring	Summer	Fall	Winter
March	June	September	December
April	July	October	January
May	August	November	February

Spring months are warm.	*Summer months are hot.*	*Fall months are cool.*	*Winter months are cold.*

(*Note*: In some parts of the world, the summer months are December, January, and February. The winter months are June, July, and August.)

☛ Practice: "Are the winter months cold?"

1. S1: Are the winter months cold here?
    S2: Yes, they are.

2. S1: Is it cold in the spring?
    S2: No, it isn't. It's warm.

Let's Talk: You Need a Heavy Jacket

It's October. Sara and Tomas are looking at their winter clothes.

Sara: Tomas, let's go shopping. You need a jacket.

Tomas: No, I don't. That's a new jacket.

Sara: This jacket is very light. You need a heavy jacket for winter.

Tomas: Oh, all right. But I don't like to go shopping.

☞ Practice: "What do you need?"

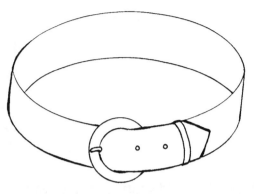

1. S1: What do you need?
    S2: I need a new shirt.

2. S1: What does Lisa need?
    S2: She needs a wide belt.

3. S1: Do you want a new dress?
    S2: No, I don't. I want a new skirt.

4. S1: Does she want a short jacket?
    S2: No, she doesn't.
         She wants a long coat.

5. S1: What does Joe have?
    S2: He has a new suit.
    S1: What does he want?
    S2: He wants a new tie.

6. S1: What does Sara want?
    S2: She wants a light jacket.
    S1: What does she need?
    S2: She needs a heavy jacket.

■ Interaction: Talk about the Weather

1. Discuss the weather and seasons.

Do you like cold weather or hot weather?

What season do you like best?

Do you like the weather in your city?

What kind of clothing do you need for summer?

What do you need for winter?

2. Tell the class about the people in your group.

Examples: *Rita* likes the *winter* months.

She likes *cold* weather.

She wants *a short dress* for summer.

She needs *a heavy jacket* for winter.

Reading: At the Department Store

Sara and Tomas are in the men's section of the department store.

Salesman: May I help you?

Tomas: I need a jacket.

Salesman: We have a sale
on jackets today.

Tomas: I need a heavy jacket
for winter.

Salesman: Here's a warm jacket.
Try it on.

Discussion

1. Where are Sara and Tomas?
2. What do they want to buy?
3. Why does Tomas need a new jacket?
4. Do you like to go shopping? Why?
5. How often do you go shopping?
6. Where do you like to shop for clothing?

✍ Writing

1. Where are Tomas and Sara?

   _____.

2. _____?

   He needs a jacket.

3. What kind of jacket _____?

   He needs a _____ jacket for _____.

4. What's on sale?

   _____ are on sale.

✍✍ More Writing

Make two shopping lists for clothing.

I want...	I need...
_____	_____
_____	_____
_____	_____

A. Write about Greta's closet.

| belt | closet | doesn't | dress | heavy | light | needs | skirt | shirts |

This is Greta's _____. There aren't many clothes. There's a long

_____ and a short _____. There are two old

_____ and a narrow _____. There are two

jackets. One is _____, and the other is _____.

Greta _____ like to go shopping, but she _____

some new clothes!

B. Write a question for the answer.

1. Is it cold in the spring?

   _____ *No, it isn't* _____. It's warm.

2. _____?

   No, I don't. I need a heavy coat.

3. Does she want a short dress?

   _____. _____a long dress.

4. _____he like the summer months?

   No, _____. He _____ the winter months.

5. _____ they like cold weather?

   No, _____. _____the hot summer months.

She's Wearing a White Dress

Objectives: In this lesson you will learn to talk about what is happening now. You will also learn the colors.

✔ Review: The Seasons and Clothing

1. Write the four seasons on the board.
    Write the months of each season.
2. Discuss the different seasons in your countries.
    How is the weather in each season?
    Do you wear different clothing for different seasons?

Something New: What Am I Doing Now?
Listen and Look

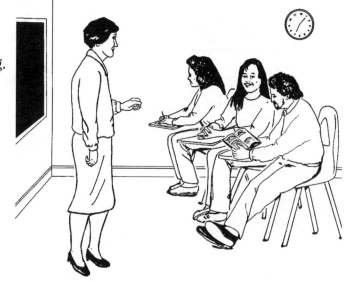

Mrs. Baker:	I'm standing and talking.
May:	I'm listening.
Tony:	I'm reading.
Sara:	I'm writing.
May, Tony, and Sara:	We're sitting.

☛ Practice: "She's listening"

1. S1: What's May doing?
   S2: She's listening.

2. S1: What's Tony doing?
   S2: He's reading.

3. S1: Is Mrs. Baker reading?
   S2: No, she isn't. She's talking.

4. S1: Is Sara talking?
   S2: No, she isn't. She's writing.

☛ Practice Activity: What are they doing?

Six students show the following actions:
   sitting, standing, talking, listening, reading, writing

Ask and answer questions about what the students are doing.

Examples: S1: What's David doing?
   S2: He's listening.
   S3: What is Lila doing?
   S4: She's writing. Etc.

Let's Talk: She's Wearing a White Dress

Maria Garcia and her daughter Gina are shopping today. While Maria is looking at jewelry, Gina walks away.

Maria: Gina! Where are you?

Manager: May I help you?

Maria: Yes, I'm looking for my little girl.

Manager: Please describe her to me.

Maria: She's six years old and she's wearing a white dress.

Manager: There she is. She's looking at the toys.

☞ Practice: "She's wearing a black sweater"

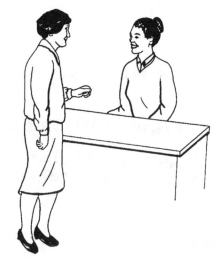

1. S1: What's she wearing?
    S2: She's wearing a black sweater.

2. S1: What's Mrs. Baker doing?
    S2: She's talking to the salesclerk.

Something New: Colors

Listen and Look

Who is wearing these colors? Write their names on the chart.

color	student	color	student
red		green	
orange		blue	
yellow		purple	
brown		black	
white			

☛ Practice Activity: What are they wearing?

Write the names of students in class and draw a line to the color and the clothing they are wearing.

Name	Color	Clothing
Sue	red	shirt
	orange	dress
	white	jacket
	black	coat
	blue	skirt
	yellow	belt
	purple	shoes
	brown	blouse
	green	sweater

Reading: At the Shopping Mall

Linda and Lucy are at the shopping mall today. They are looking at blouses at a department store. A saleslady is helping them. "We're having a sale today," says the saleslady. "They're only 15 dollars." Linda and Lucy don't need new blouses, but 15 dollars is a good price.

Discussion

1. Where are Linda and Lucy today?
2. What are they doing there?
3. What's on sale today?
4. Do they need new blouses?
5. Are they buying new blouses?
6. Do you like to go shopping?

✍ Writing

Fill in the blanks:

1. Are the students standing?

   No, _____.

   What are they doing?

   _____.

2. _____ wearing a brown jacket?

   No, he isn't.

   _____?

   He's wearing a _____.

3. Are you looking for a sweater?

   No, _____.

   What are you looking for?

   _____ a blouse.

4. Is she writing?

   No, _____.

   _____?

   She's reading.

A. Listen and circle the correct picture.

1.

a.   b.   c.

2.

a.   b.   c.

3.

a.   b.   c.

4.

a.   b.   c.

B. Draw a picture of yourself today. Write about what you're wearing.

Example: I'm wearing a white shirt, a black belt, black pants, white socks, and black shoes.

Now draw a picture of a student in class. Write about his or her clothes.

Example: This is my friend. He's wearing a red shirt, brown pants, and brown shoes.

Now show your picture to other students. See if they can guess who is in your picture.

C. Match the question with the answer.

_____ 1. What do you need?   a. Yes, they are.

_____ 2. What color do you want?   b. It's $40.00.

_____ 3. How much is that jacket?   c. I need a light jacket.

_____ 4. Are those jackets on sale? d. Yes, I do.

_____ 5. How much are they?   e. Black.

_____ 6. Do you want a new jacket?   f. $29.95.

D. Look at the picture with your group and write a conversation. Choose people to act out the conversation for the class.

Write your conversation here:

_____

_____

_____

_____

_____

_____

_____

_____

_____

Lesson 36

He's Watching TV

Objectives: In this lesson you will learn to talk about family and household activities.

✔ Review: Colors and Actions

1. Name the colors of the rainbow.
2. Find students who are wearing these colors and identify the clothing.
3. Talk about what they are doing right now.

Something New: Saturday Activities

Listen and Look

Saturday is a busy day in the Garcia family. What is the family doing?

Maria is cleaning the house.

Jim is mowing the lawn.

Luisa and Cecilia are doing the dishes.

Luisa is washing the dishes.   Cecilia is drying the dishes.

Salsa is running around.

☞ Practice: "He's mowing the lawn"

1. S1: What's Jim doing?
   S2: He's mowing the lawn.

2. S1: What's Maria doing?
   S2: She's vacuuming the carpet.

3. S1: Is Salsa helping?
   S2: No, he isn't.
   S1: What's he doing?
   S2: He's running around.

4. S1: Are the girls studying?
   S2: No, they aren't.
   S1: What are they doing?
   S2: They're doing the dishes.

Let's Talk: He's Watching TV

Elsa and Ricardo Soto are calling their babysitter from a restaurant.

Ricardo: Hi, Luisa. How are the children?

Luisa: They're fine, Mr. Soto.

Ricardo: What's Roberto doing?

Luisa: He's watching TV.

Ricardo: Is Rita watching TV, too?

Luisa: No, she isn't. She's sleeping in the bedroom.

Ricardo: That's good. See you at 11.

Luisa: Okay.

☛ Practice: "He's in the living room"

1. S1: Where's Roberto?
   S2: He's in the living room.
   S1: What's he doing?
   S2: He's watching TV.

2. S1: Where's Rita?
   S2: She's in the bedroom.
   S1: What's she doing?
   S2: She's sleeping.

3. S1: Are Elsa and Ricardo at home?
   S2: No, they aren't.
   S1: Where are they?
   S2: They're at a restaurant.

■ Interaction: Household Activities

1. Make two lists of household activities.

Indoor jobs	Outdoor jobs
dust the furniture	*mow the lawn*

2. Take turns acting out the jobs for the class to identify.

   Examples: S1:   (Act out dusting)

         Class: You're dusting the furniture.

         S2:   (Act out mowing the lawn)

         Class: You're mowing the lawn.

Reading: Babysitters

Elsa and Ricardo have a baby daughter and a five–year–old son. They like to go to the theater or to a restaurant on weekends. They can't take the children, so they hire a babysitter. Luisa is their babysitter. She is a teenage neighbor. She likes the children and they like her. She is saving her money for college.

Discussion

1. What do Elsa and Ricardo like to do on weekends?
2. Why do they need a babysitter?
3. What does a babysitter need to do?
4. Do you think Luisa enjoys her job? Why?
5. Do you have little children? If so, who babysits for you?

✎ Writing

Write about the people in the picture.

1. *The father is mowing the lawn.*

2. *The mother*

3.

4.

5.

A. *Talk about the picture.*

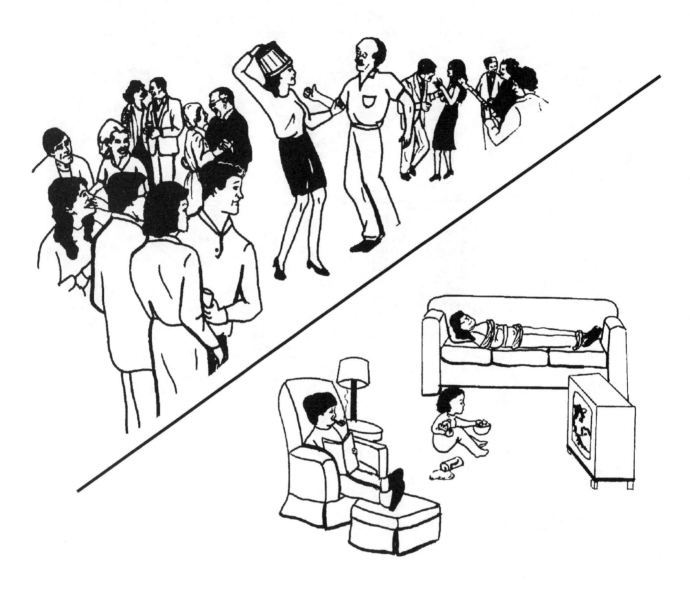

B. Write questions or answers about the picture on page 108.

1. _____?

   They're in the living room.

2. What's the boy doing?

   _____.

3. _____?

   She's watching TV and eating popcorn.

4. Where's the babysitter?

   _____.

5. Is the babysitter watching the children?

   _____.

6. _____?

   They're at a party.

7. _____?

   He's talking and watching his wife.

8. What's his wife doing?

   _____.

C. Roleplay: The Parents Come Home.

1. Work in a group of five.
2. Take the role of the wife, husband, babysitter, son or daughter from the picture on page 108.
3. Decide what to say, practice with your group, and show your roleplay to the class.

Questions	Answers
What's happening here?	*I'm just eating.*

Unit Twelve **Evaluation**

I. Listening Comprehension

Listen and circle the correct answer, A or B.

1.

   A   B

2.

   A   B

3.

   A   B

4.

   A   B

5. A

   B

6.

   A   B

7.
A. No, it doesn't.

B. No, it isn't.

8.
A. Yes, she does.

B. Yes, she is.

II. Reading

Circle the correct answers.

1. Sue _____ a short skirt.

      has   have   want

2. Does Tomas _____ a new jacket?

      has   have   needs

3. _____ he doing?

      Is   Does   What's

4. Is she dusting? Yes, she _____.

      is   does   dusts

III. Writing

Complete the questions or answers.

1. a. Are the girls listening to the teacher?

   No, _____.

   b. What are they doing?

   _____.

2. a. Where's the baby?

   He's _____.

   b. _____?
   He's sleeping.

3. a. _____ she want a blouse?

   No,_____.

   b. What _____ she looking for?

   She _____ a dress.

112

Delta's Apple Pie, Book 1B

Unit Thirteen

Workers, Drivers, and Pedestrians

STUDENT DRIVER

How's Your New Job?

Objectives: In this lesson you will learn to talk about things that you are learning to do.

✔ Review: Household Activities

1. One student act out a job you do at home.
   Another student write the action on the board.
2. One student choose a job from the list and act it out.
   Practice asking and answering the question, *"What is he/she doing?"*

Something New: I'm Learning to Do Many Things
Listen and Look

I'm learning to sew.   I'm learning to bake.
I'm sewing a dress.   I'm baking bread.

He's learning to type.
He's typing a letter.

I'm learning to paint.
I'm painting a house.

I'm learning to drive a truck.
I'm driving a big truck now.

She's learning to sell jewelry.
She's selling watches.

☛ **Practice: "What are you learning to do?"**

1. S1: What are you learning to do?
   S2: I'm learning to paint houses.

2. S1: What is she learning to do?
   S2: She's learning to sew dresses.

3. S1: Is he learning to bake cakes?
   S2: No, he isn't. He's learning to bake bread.

4. S1: Is she learning to make jewelry?
   S2: No, she isn't. She's learning to sell jewelry.

Let's Talk: How's Your New Job?

Cecilia Garcia has a new job in the school office. Her husband Jim is asking about her first day at work.

Jim: How's your new job?

Cecilia: It's fun. I'm enjoying it very much.

Jim: Are you learning to do some new things?

Cecilia: Yes, I am. I'm learning to answer the telephone and to type letters, too.

☛ **Practice: "It's a lot of fun!"**

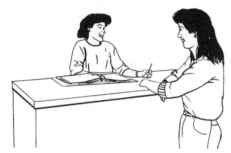

1. S1: Are you enjoying your new job?
   S2: Yes, I am. It's a lot of fun.

2. S1: Are you enjoying your new job?
   S2: Yes, I am. It's great.

3. S1: Is he enjoying his new job?
   S2: Yes, he is.
   S1: What's he doing?
   S2: He's driving a big truck.

4. S1: Is he enjoying his new job?
   S2: No, he isn't.
   S1: What's he doing?
   S2: He's painting houses.

■ Interaction: Are You Enjoying Your (New) Job?

1. If you have a new job, tell the class about it.

   S1: How's your new job?

   S2: It's great/terrible!

   S1: Are you learning to do anything new?

   S2: - .

2. If no one has a new job, talk about your jobs.

   S1: How's your job?

   S2: It's great/okay/terrible.

   S1: Are you learning to do anything new?

   S2: Yes/No, - - - - - - - - - - - - - - - - - .

★ Something Extra: Learning for Fun

She's learning to play the guitar.

They're learning to play ping–pong.

He's learning to paint pictures.

I'm learning to swim.

We're learning to cook
Chinese food.

He's learning to build
a bookcase.

■ Interaction: I'm Learning Something New

1. Talk with a partner about something you are learning to do now.
2. Tell the class what your partner is learning to do.

Reading: Lifelong Learning

Adults can attend public schools for adults all their lives. There are many kinds of classes in these schools. Some classes are for job training. Some are for general education. Some are just for fun.

Discussion

1. What does "Lifelong Learning" mean?
2. What are some job training classes?
3. What are some general education classes?
4. What are some "fun" classes?

✍ Writing

Write the questions or answers.

1. Where are there classes for adults in your city?

   _____.

2. Name three kinds of classes in adult schools:

   _____   _____   _____

3. _____ now?

   I'm learning to play the guitar.

4. What are they learning to do?

   _____.

5. _____?

   She's learning to sew.

☞ Practice Activity: Classes

1. With the help of the teacher, look over the schedule of classes for your school or a nearby adult learning center.
2. Choose classes that you would like to attend.

A. Listen and write the room number under the picture.

Room _____

Room _____

Room _____

Room _____

Room _____

Room _____

B. Look at the pictures on page 120 and write the answers below.

1. What are they doing in room 106?

   They're learning to sew.

2. What are they doing in room 105?

   _____

3. What are they doing in room 104?

   _____

4. What are they doing in room 103?

   _____

5. What are they doing in room 102?

   _____

6. What are they doing in room 101?

   _____

I'm Making a Right Turn

Objectives: In this lesson you will learn some driving actions. You will also learn about rules for pedestrians.

✔ Review: Learning New Activities

1. Are you learning to do something new at work?
2. Are you learning to do anything just for fun?
3. Tell the class what you are learning to do. If you can, show the class what you are learning or act out how to do it (play the guitar, knit, etc.).

Something New: Learning to Drive

Listen and Look

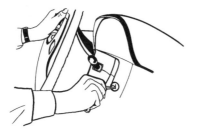

I'm starting the car.

I'm shifting.

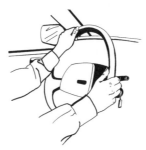

I'm steering.

I'm pulling out.

I'm making a right turn.

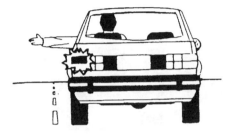

I'm making a left turn.

I'm slowing down.

I'm stopping.

I'm parking.

☞ Practice Activity: Driving actions

1. One student act out a driving action and say the action you are doing.

    S1: (Acts out steering) I'm *steering*.

2. Ask and answer questions about the action.

    S2: What's she doing?

    S3: She's *steering*.

Let's Talk: I'm Making a Right Turn

Jae Kim is taking a driving lesson.

Mr. Young: What are you doing, Mrs. Kim?

Jae Kim: I'm making a right turn.

Mr. Young: You're giving a left turn signal.

Jae Kim: Oops! (Changes her arm signal.)

Mr. Young: That's good.

☞ Practice: "What are you doing?"

1. S1: What are you doing?

    S2: I'm starting the car.

2. S1: Is he making a right turn or a left turn?

    S2: He's making a left turn.

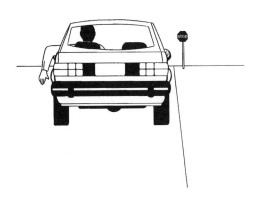
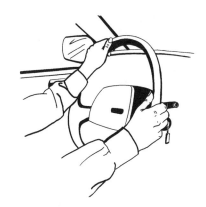

3. S1: Is he shifting?
    S2: No, he isn't. He's slowing down.

4. S1: What is he doing?
    S2: He's steering.

Something New: Rules for Drivers and Pedestrians

Listen and Look

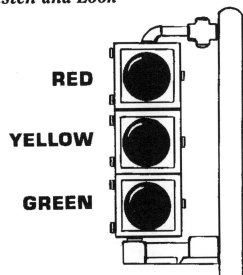

RED

YELLOW

GREEN

For drivers:
A red light means **STOP**.
A yellow light means **SLOW DOWN**.
A green light means **GO**.

For pedestrians:
A red light means **STOP**.
A yellow light means **WAIT**.
A green light means **GO**.

CROSS the street.

DON'T CROSS the street.

■ Interaction: Traffic Signals

With a partner, ask and answer questions about the traffic signals. Use the question, *What does... mean?*

Examples:

S1: What does *a red light* mean?

S2: It means *stop*.

S1: What does *walk* mean?

S2: It means *cross the street*. Etc.

Reading: Pedestrians

Here is an intersection. There are four crosswalks for pedestrians.

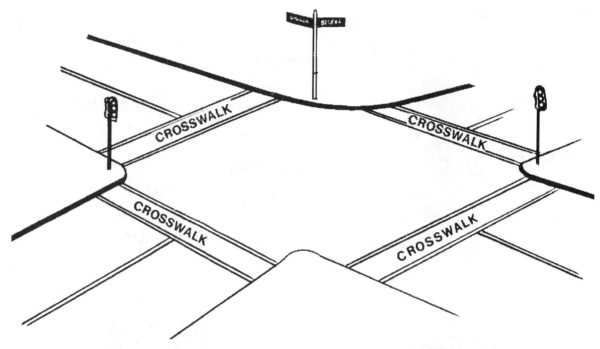

In some cities, people only cross the street at intersections. People only cross on green lights. In other cities, people don't use crosswalks. They cross anywhere, and they don't get tickets!

Discussion

1. What does a driver need to know?
2. What does a pedestrian need to know?
3. How do pedestrians cross in your city?

✐ Writing

Write the questions or answers.

1. What is an important rule for pedestrians?

   _____ .

2. Are there traffic lights for both pedestrians and drivers?

   _____ .

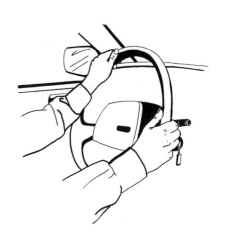

3. Is he starting the car?

   _____ .

4. What's he doing?

   _____ .

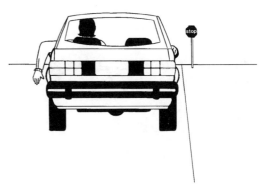

5. Is she shifting?

   _____ .

6. _____ ?

   She's slowing down.

Lesson 38 Activity Pages

A. Match the picture to the sentence.

_____1. He's making a right turn.   _____3. He's pulling out.

_____2. He's making a left turn.   _____4. He's stopping.

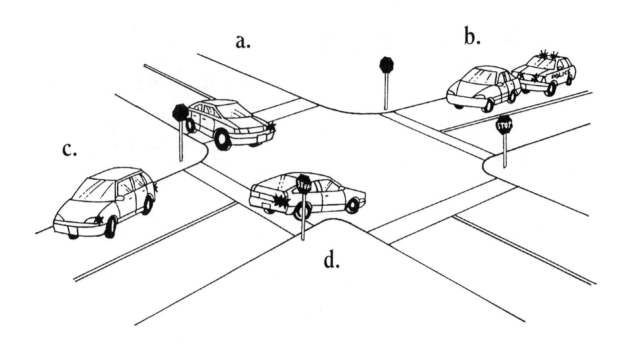

B. Put the sentences in order. Then say the sentences and give your partner a driving lesson.

_____ Drive the car.

_____ Signal left.

_____ Start the car.

_____ Pull out.

_____ Put on your seatbelt.

_____ Look in the mirror.

_____ Look over your left shoulder.

Delta's Apple Pie, Book 1B

C. What does this mean? Complete the sentences.

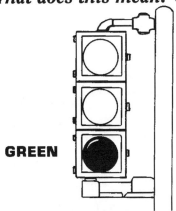

GREEN

1. For drivers this means _*go*_____.

2. For pedestrians this means _____.

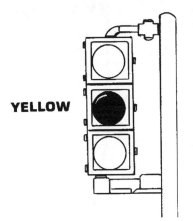

YELLOW

3. For drivers this means _____.

4. For pedestrians this means _____.

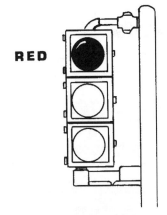

RED

5. For drivers this means _____.

6. For pedestrians this means _____.

7. For pedestrians this means _____

_____.

D. Talk about the picture.

E. Read the conversation.

Practice with your friends. Act out the conversation for the class.

Police Officer: Good morning. May I see your license?

Mr. Kim: Yes, officer. Here it is.

Police Officer: Your left signal light isn't working.

Mr. Kim: Really? I'm sorry.

Police Officer: Please fix it right away. I'm not writing a ticket this time.

Mr. Kim: Thank you, officer.

Mrs. Kim: Yes, thank you, officer. My husband is teaching me to drive.

Police Officer: Good luck, Ma'am!

F. Match the questions to the answers.

_e_ 1. Is Mrs. Kim driving?

a. The left signal isn't working.

_____ 2. Who is driving the car?

b. No, he isn't.

_____ 3. Who is talking to Mr. Kim?

c. Mr. Kim.

_____ 4. What's the matter?

d. No, she doesn't.

_____ 5. Is the police officer writing a ticket?

e. No, she isn't.

_____ 6. Does Mrs. Kim have a driver's license?

f. The police officer.

Lesson 39

I'm Studying the Driving Rules

Objective: In this lesson you will learn how to get a driver's license.

✔ Review: Following Directions

One student be a driving teacher and give directions. Another student follow the directions.

>   ***Examples:*** S1: *Start the car.*
>
>   S2: (Act out starting a car.)
>
>   S1: *Pull out*
>
>   S2: (Act out pulling out.)

Something New: I Want a Driver's License
Listen and Look

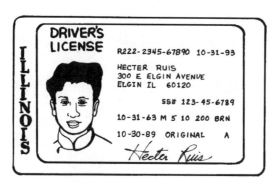

I need a driver's license.

What do I need to do?

I need to learn the traffic signs.

I need to learn to drive.

I need to take a test.

☛ Practice: "What does she need to do?"

Jae Kim wants to learn to drive.

1. S1: What does she need to do?
   S2: She needs to learn to drive.

2. S1: What does she need to do?
   S2: She needs to learn the traffic signs.

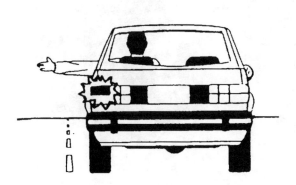

3. S1: I want to make a left turn.
   What do I need to do?

   S2: You need to make a left turn signal.

4. S1: He needs to take a driving test.
   What does he need to do?

   S2: He needs to study the driving rules.

Let's Talk: I'm Studying the Driving Rules

Jae Kim is studying for her driving test during her lunch hour at work.

Mark: What are you reading, Jae?

Jae: I'm studying the driving rules.

Mark: Are they very difficult?

Jae: Yes, they are. But I know the traffic signs now.

☞ **Practice: "She's studying the driving rules"**

1. S1: What's Anna doing?
   S2: She's studying the driving rules.

2. S1: What are you studying?
   S2: I'm studying the traffic signs.

3. S1: Are the rules difficult?
   S2: Yes, they are.

4. S1: Are the signs difficult?
   S2: No, they aren't.

★ Something Extra: More Road Signs

The speed limit is 45 miles an hour.

Slow down to 25 miles an hour.

☞ Practice: "There's a school sign"

1. S1: There's a SCHOOL sign.
   What does he need to do?

   S2: Slow down.

2. S1: There's a STOP sign.
   What does she need to do?

   S2: Slow down and stop.

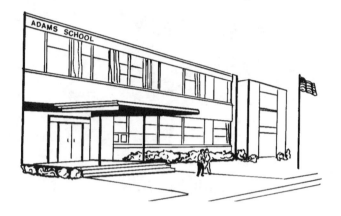

3. S1: He's driving 50 miles an hour.
   What does he need to do?

   S2: He needs to slow down.

4. S1: What's the speed limit near a
   school?

   S2: It's 25 miles an hour.

■ Interaction: A Driving Test

1. Give the arm signals.

   S1: Make a left turn.

   S2: (Signals a left turn.)

   S1: Make a right turn.

   S2: (Signals a right turn.) Etc.

2. Draw the traffic signs.

        S1: What's the "STOP" sign?

        S2: (Draws the STOP sign.)

        S1: What's the "No Right Turn" sign?

        S2: (Draws the correct sign.) Etc.

Reading: Driver Education

Teenagers love cars. They want to learn to drive. They want to own a car. There are driver education classes in many high schools. There are also many driving classes. Students need a learner's permit to learn to drive.

Discussion

1. What do teenagers want to do?
2. How can teenagers learn to drive?
3. What is a learner's permit?
4. Why do you think teenagers love cars so much?

✍ Writing

Fill in the blanks.

1. I want a driver's license. What do I need to do?

    a. You need to learn the _____ rules.

    b. You need to learn the _____ signs.

    c. You need to learn to _____.

    d. You need to take a _____.

Write the questions or answers.

2. What's Jae learning?

    She's _____.

3. There's a STOP sign. What does she need to do?

    She _____.

4. There's a SCHOOL sign.

    _____?

    He needs to slow down.

A. Ask and answer questions about the people.

Work with a partner.

Name	What does _____ want to do?	What does _____ need to do?
Jae	drive	get a license
Pat	make birthday cakes	learn to bake
Carl	get a job	learn English
Fran	paint houses	find customers
Your Partner	?	?

B. Look at the information in A and write the answers.

1. What does Jae need to do?

   She needs to get a driver's license.

2. What does Carl need to do?

   _____

3. What does Pat need to do?

   _____

4. What does Fran need to do?

   _____

5. What does your partner want to do?

   _____

6. What does your partner need to do?

   _____

C. Look for someone who...

Ask and answer the question, *"Do you need to _____?"*
If a student answers *"Yes"* write his/her name next to the question.

Question   **Name**

1. ...get a job?   _____

2. ...learn to drive?   _____

3. ...learn to speak English?   _____

4. _____?   _____

5. _____?   _____

6. _____?   _____

7. _____?   _____

8. _____?   _____

D. Now write three sentences about the students you talked to.

Example: Rosa needs to learn to sew.

1. _____

2. _____

3. _____

Unit Thirteen

I. Listening Comprehension

Listen and circle the correct answer, A or B.

1.

   A   B

2.

   A   B

3.

   A   B

4.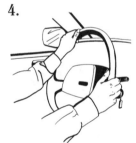

   A   B

5.

   A. Yes, I do.
   B. Yes, I am.

6.

   A   B

II. Reading

Circle the correct answers.

1. What's she _____ to do?

   learns   learning   to learn

2. The rules are _____.

   slow   red   difficult

3. There _____ classes for
   adults in public schools.

   drive   is   are

4. Pedestrians must _____
   traffic signals, too.

   wait   know   cross

III. Writing

Write the correct words in the blanks.

Sam is _____ to school. He

wants to _____ to drive.

There is a driver _____ class

at his school. He is a _____ in

the class.

on
at
teacher
driving
learn
learning
walking
student
education

Unit Fourteen

The World of Work

I Take the Bus to Work Every Day

Objectives: In this lesson you will learn to talk about daily activities.

✔ Review: Information for Drivers

Driver's License

1. Make a list of what a person needs to do to get a driver's license.
2. Put the steps in order.

Traffic Signs

1. Draw the traffic signs on the board, or use the signs below.
2. Ask and answer questions about what they mean.

> **Example:**   What does this (sign) mean?
>
>   It means no left turn.

Something New: I Work Every Day
Listen and Look

I'm getting up.
I get up at 6:00 every day.

I'm eating breakfast.
I eat breakfast every morning.

I'm leaving the house.
I leave at 7:00 every morning.

I'm walking.
I walk to the bus stop every day.

I'm taking the bus.
I take the bus to work every day.

I'm working.
I work in an office downtown.

☞ Practice: "She's getting up"

1. S1: What's she doing now?
    S2: She's getting up.
    S1: What time does she get up every morning?
    S2: She gets up at 6:00.

2. S1: What's she doing now?
    S2: She's leaving the house.
    S1: When does she leave the house every day?
    S2: She leaves at 7:00.

Let's Talk: I Take the Bus to Work Every Day

Tomas sees Jae at the bus stop.

Tomas: Hi, how are you?

Jae: Fine, thank you.

Tomas: Are you waiting for the #4 bus, too?

Jae: Yes, I am. I take it to work every day.

Tomas: Where do you work?

Jae: I work downtown.

☛ Practice Activity: What do you do every day?

Ask and answer questions about what people in class do every day.
Each person say something different.

★ Something Extra: Regular Activities

Every day

brush my teeth

take a shower

comb my hair

Every Weekend

eat at a restaurant

visit my family

go to the movies

☞ Practice Activity: Daily activities, weekend activities

1. Ask and answer questions about what you do every day and every weekend.
2. Record the answers on a grid.

Name	Every day	Every weekend
Alberto	works in a garage	goes to the bank

☞ Practice Activity: What are you doing?

One student act out an activity from the grid above.

Another student ask: "What are you doing?"

"Do you _____ every day/every weekend?"

Reading: Every Day Is the Same

Every day is the same for me. I get up early. I run in the park in good weather. I exercise at home in bad weather. I take a shower and wash my hair every day. Then I make coffee and breakfast. I eat and get ready to leave. I go to work on weekdays, but I go out on Saturdays and Sundays.

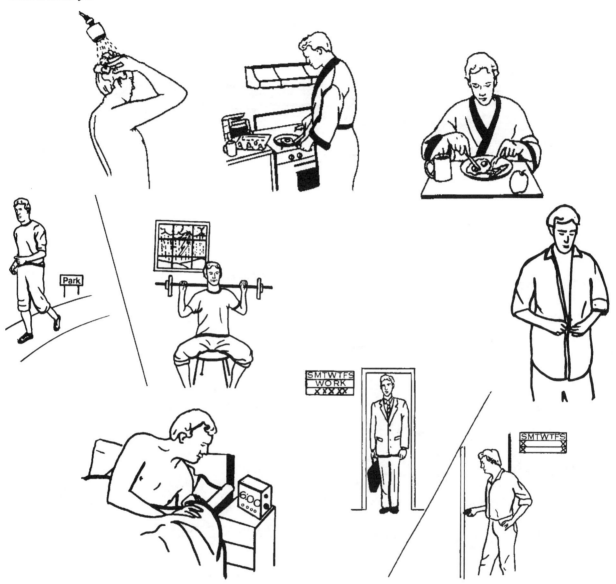

Discussion

1. Do you get up early?
2. Do you like to run?
3. Do you exercise?
4. Do you drink coffee?
5. Do you eat breakfast every morning?
6. What days do you work?
7. Do you go out on Saturdays and Sundays?

✑ Writing

Use the information in the Reading to fill in the blanks.

1. He _____ early every day.

2. He runs _____ the park in good weather.

3. In bad weather he _____ at home.

4. He _____ a shower every day.

5. He _____ his hair every day.

6. He _____ breakfast and then

   _____ ready for work.

7. He goes to work _____ weekdays.

8. He goes out _____ Saturdays and Sundays.

★ Something Extra: Your Own Writing

Use some of these words to write about what you do every day.

get up	run	go to work
take a shower	exercise	drive
take a bath	make breakfast	take the bus
brush my teeth	eat	work
brush my hair	drink	go out

_____

_____

_____

_____

_____

_____

_____

_____

_____

Lesson 40 Activity Pages

A. Listen to the sentence and check Now or Every...

✔	Now	Every...
1.		
2.		
3.		
4.		
5.		
6.		

B. Group Grid

Form a group.

Ask and answer the questions. Write the short answers on the grid.

Every...	day	week	month	year
Once a...	day	week	month	year
Three times a...	day	week	month	year

Name	How often do you...				
	come to school?	watch TV?	go to the movies?	eat pizza?	cut your hair?

Lesson 41

Where Do You Work?

Objectives: In this lesson you will learn to say where you work and what you do at work.

✔ Review: Regular Activities

1. Ask your partner to name one thing he or she does every day and one thing he or she does every weekend.
2. Report to the class.

   Example: _____ brushes his teeth every day.

   He runs in the park every weekend.

Something New: I Work at a Video Store

I work at a video store.

He works at the post office.

They work for a moving company.

They don't work. They're students.

We don't work. We're retired.

She works at home. She's a homemaker.

☛ **Practice: "Where does he work?"**

1. S1: Where does he work?
   S2: He works at the post office.

2. S1: Where do they work?
   S2: They work for a moving company.

Let's Talk: Do You Work Every Day?

Tony and May are talking during a class break.

Tony: Do you have a job?

May: Yes, I do. I work at Super Save.

Tony: Do you work every day?

May: No, I don't. I work

six days a week.

Tony: Oh, you work six days a

week! When's your day off?

May: It's Monday.

☛ **Practice: "How many days a week does she work?"**

SUN.	MON.	TUES.	WED.	THURS.	FRI.	SAT.
	✕	✕	✕	✕	✕	

1. S1: Does she work every day?
    S2: No, she doesn't.
    S1: How many days a week does she work?
    S2: She works Monday through Friday.

SUN.	MON.	TUES.	WED.	THURS.	FRI.	SAT.
	✕	✕	✕	✕	✕	✕

2. S1: How many days a week does he work?
    S2: He works six days.
    S1: When is his day off?
    S2: It's Sunday.

★ Something Extra: Time Cards

COMPANY			
Imports International			
NAME			
George Hee			

Sunday	IN			
	OUT			
	IN			
	OUT			
Saturday	IN			
	OUT			
	IN			
	OUT			
Friday	IN		*7:30*	
	OUT			
	IN			
	OUT		*4:30*	
Thursday	IN		*7:30*	
	OUT			
	IN			
	OUT		*4:30*	
Wednesday	IN		*7:30*	
	OUT			
	IN			
	OUT		*4:30*	
Tuesday	IN		*7:30*	
	OUT			
	IN			
	OUT		*4:30*	
Monday	IN		*7:30*	
	OUT			
	IN			
	OUT		*4:30*	

1. This is a time card for_____ .

2. He works from _____ to _____ .

3. His days off are _____ and _____ .

4. He starts work at _____ .

5. He finishes work at _____ .

☛ Practice Activity: My time card

Fill in your time card for one week. Fill in:

1. Your name.
2. The name of your company.
3. The time you begin and finish work.

(Don't fill in your day or days off.)

COMPANY			
NAME			

Week ____ to ____	Monday	IN		
		OUT		
		IN		
		OUT		
	Tuesday	IN		
		OUT		
		IN		
		OUT		
	Wednesday	IN		
		OUT		
		IN		
		OUT		
	Thursday	IN		
		OUT		
		IN		
		OUT		
	Friday	IN		
		OUT		
		IN		
		OUT		
	Saturday	IN		
		OUT		
		IN		
		OUT		
	Sunday	IN		
		OUT		
		IN		
		OUT		

■ Interaction: What Days Do You Work?

Ask your classmates about their jobs:

1. Do you have a job?
2. Where do you work?
3. What days do you work?
4. What time do you begin work? What time do you finish?
5. When are your days off?
6. Do you like your job?

★ Something Extra: What Do You Do at Work?

I use a computer to type letters.

I file.

I answer the phone.

I take messages.

Reading: My New Job

Dear Sherry,

I'm sitting in the lunchroom now. I'm eating lunch and writing a letter to you. How are you? I hope you and your family are fine.

My new job is fine. I work in an office. I am learning to use a computer. I use a computer to type letters. I also file, answer the phone, and take messages.

The people in the office are friendly, and I like them. Well, I need to say "Good-bye" now. It's time for me to go back to work. Please write soon.

Love,
Gloria

Discussion

1. Where's Gloria?
2. What time is it?
3. What is she doing?
4. Is Gloria learning something new at work?
5. What does she do at work?
6. Does Gloria have a good job?

✍ Writing

Fill in the blanks with the words below:

answers	files	likes	takes
are	is	office	uses
computer	job	pay	

Gloria Polsky is an _____ clerk. It's a new _____ for Gloria.

She _____ the job. The people in the office _____ friendly.

She _____ learning to use a _____. She _____

the computer to type letters. She also files, _____ the phone, and

_____ messages.

✍✍ More Writing

Write about yourself and your job.

_____

_____

_____

_____

_____

_____

A. Listen and match the job with the name.

1. Joe   _____ student

2. Martha   _____ truck driver

3. Teresa   _____ doctor

4. Victor   _____ homemaker

5. Ken   _____ secretary

6. Yvonne   _____ plumber

B. Ask and answer questions about the missing information.

Partner A look at page 162. Partner B look at page 163.

Partner A: Ask: *When does Teresa start/finish work?*
What does Joe do at 10:00?/at 4:00? Etc.

Worker	Start	10:00 AM	12:00 PM	4:00 PM	Finish
Teresa	?	?	give the baby lunch	pick up the children	?
Joe	8:00 AM	?	eat lunch	?	5:00 PM

Partner B: Ask: *When does Joe start/finish work?*
What does Teresa do at 12:00?/at 4:00? Etc.

Worker	Start	10:00 AM	12:00 PM	4:00 PM	Finish
Teresa	6 AM	clean the house	?	?	11:30 PM
Joe	?	answer phones	?	type letters	?

C. What do you think?

What is Teresa's job? _____

What is Joe's job? _____

D. Talk about the picture below.

E. Read the story and complete the sentences.

delivers	English	break	types
typing	go	starts	secretary

This is the ABC Pillow Factory. You can see some of the people in the factory. Mr.

Mendez, the truck driver, is taking a _____. He

_____ work at 6:00 a.m. every morning. He

_____ pillows to department stores. Ms. Sanchez is a

_____. She's _____ a letter right

now. She _____ 30 or 40 letters every day!

The workers at the ABC Pillow Factory like their jobs. The hours are good and the

people are nice. After work, many workers _____ to school to learn

_____ .

F. Write the questions or the answers.

1. Is Mr. Mendez a secretary?

   _____ .

   He's _____ .

2. _____ Mr. Mendez _____ ?

   He starts work at 6:00.

3. What does Mr. Mendez do?

   _____ .

4. Is Ms. Sanchez typing?

   _____ .

   _____ a letter.

5. _____ 30 to 40 letters every day?

   Yes, she does.

6. Do the workers at ABC like their jobs?

   _____ .

7. What do many workers do after work?

   _____ .

   _____ .

Lesson 42

He Paints Cars at Work

Objectives: In this lesson you will learn to talk about things people do at work, at home, and at school.

✔ **Review:** What I Do Every Day

Ask your classmates what they do every day.

Examples: What do you do every morning?

What do you do at work every day?

What do you do every evening?

Something New: Workday Activities

Listen and Look

The alarm is ringing.
It rings at 6:00 every day.

Tom's putting on his shirt.
He wears a uniform at work.

He's getting on the freeway.
He takes the freeway to work.

He's looking for a parking space.
He parks in the "Compact Car" section.

He's signing in.
He starts work at 8:00.

He's wearing a safety mask.
He paints cars at work.

☛ Practice Activity: What time does he get up?

Hold up the pictures of Tom's activities and ask and answer questions about them.

Examples: "What time does he get up?"

"What does he wear at work?"

"How does he get to work?" Etc.

Let's Talk: Grandmother's Daily Activities

Mrs. Green is asking about Alfredo's grandmother.

Mrs. Green: How's your grandmother, Alfredo?

Alfredo: Oh, she's fine, thanks.

Mrs. Green: Does she stay home every day?

Alfredo: No, she goes to the market on Fridays.

Mrs. Green: What does she do at home?

Alfredo: She cooks, washes the dishes, and does a little housework. She likes to work in the garden, too.

Discussion

1. Does Alfredo's grandmother work?
2. What does she do at home?
3. Does she ever go out?
4. What does she enjoy?
5. Do you have retired parents or grandparents?
6. How do they spend their time?

★ Something Extra: Pronunciation

/–s/ **paints**	/–z/ **stays**	/iz/ **washes**
starts	plays	brushes
gets up	enjoys	finishes
speaks	cleans	fixes
walks	signs in	kisses
types	drives	watches
sleeps	leaves	teaches

☞ Practice: "How do you say this word?"

talks	sews	teaches	sleeps
plays	writes	speaks	gets up
reads	bakes	answers	works

☛ Practice: "What does she do at work?"

Fill in the blanks to make sentences.

1. _____ letters.

2. _____ Japanese food.

3. _____ cars.

4. _____ bread.

5. _____ watches.

6. _____ a truck.

Reading: Schoolday Activities

Mr. Murphy is a teacher. Right now he is working at home. He's checking his students' homework. He really likes his job and his students. He says it's the best job in the world.

Mr. Murphy teaches children at an elementary school. He prepares lessons for them every day. He reads to them. He teaches them writing and mathematics. Sometimes they paint pictures and play music. The children have fun at school.

Discussion

1. What is Mr. Murphy's job?
2. How does he like it?
3. What does he do at home?
4. What does he do at school?
5. What does he teach the children?
6. Do the children enjoy school?

✍ Writing

Make sentences.

Mr. Murphy's activities at work:

1. He _____ .

2. _____ .

3. _____ .

The children's activities:

1. They_____ .

2. _____ .

Lesson 42 Activity Pages

A. *Listen and write yes or no.*

Maria	Felicia	George
1. _____no_____	1. _____	1. _____
2. _____	2. _____	2. _____
3. _____	3. _____	3. _____
4. _____	4. _____	4. _____

B. BINGO!!

Ask and answer DO YOU questions. Get a signature when the answer is yes. You may get only one signature from each student.

have a job	study English	get up early	get up late
_____	_____	_____	_____
eat breakfast	finish work after midnight	want to get a job	go to work at night
_____	_____	_____	_____
type at work	answer phones at work	fix things at home	speak English at work
_____	_____	_____	_____
drive	take the bus	have fun at work	have fun at school
_____	_____	_____	_____

C. Write four sentences using the information from BINGO.

Example: *Martin fixes things at home.*

1. _____

2. _____

3. _____

4. _____

D. Ask and answer the questions with a partner.

What does he do?

He's a teacher.

What does she do?

She's a doctor.

What do you do?

I'm a - - - - - - - - - - - - - - - - - .

Notes

Unit Fourteen  Evaluation

I. Listening Comprehension

Listen and circle the correct answer, A or B.

1.

    A   B

2.

    A   B

3.

    A   B

4.

    A   B

5.

    A. Yes, they are.

    B. Yes, they do.

6.

    A. No, she doesn't.

    B. No, she isn't.

II. Reading

Circle the correct answers.

1. I _____ the bus to work every day.

    leave   take   see

2. Is he _____ to the movies now?

    goes   go   going

3. May doesn't work on Mondays.
   It's her _____.

    birthday   day off   off day

4. Ken is signing in at 8:00 AM.
   He _____ work at 8:00 AM.

    finishes   signs   starts

III. Writing

1. What does she do every morning?

   _____ .

2. _____ every morning?

   He brushes his teeth.

3. Does she stay home every day?

   No, _____ on Fridays.

4. _____ ?

   She's answering the phone.

5. _____ ?

   She works in an office.

6. What does he do at work?

   _____ .

Unit Fifteen

Getting Around

It Goes West to the Mall

Objectives: In this lesson you will learn to give simple directions to various locations.

✔ Review: What Do You Do?

Ask your classmates about their jobs.
> ***Examples:*** What's your job?
> What do you do?

Tell the class about the people you talked to.
> ***Examples***: Lidia is a nurse's assistant.
> Tai is an auto mechanic.

Something New: North, South, East, and West
Listen and Look

Point to the **north** • Point to the **south** • Point to the **east** • Point to the **west**

Bus #6 is going north on Vermont.

Bus #22 is going south on Vermont.

Bus #11 is going east on Beverly.

Bus #14 is going west on Beverly.

They all go to Central Adult School at the corner of Vermont and Beverly.

☞ Practice: "Does bus #6 go to the school?"

1. S1: Does Bus #6 go to the school?
   S2: Yes, it does.

2. S1: Where is Central Adult School?
   S2: It's at the corner of Beverly and Vermont.

3. S1: Is the #11 bus going west on Beverly?
   S2: No, it isn't. It's going east.

4. S1: Where does the #22 bus go?
   S2: It goes south on Vermont.

Let's Talk: It Goes to the Mall

May and Maria are talking at the break. They are making plans for the weekend.

May: Let's go shopping on Saturday.

Maria: Okay. Shall we go to the new mall?

May: All right. What bus do I take? Do you know?

Maria: Take the #4 bus. It goes west on Lincoln to the mall. Get off at Madison.

May: Okay. See you there.

☞ Practice: "What bus do I take?"

1. S1: What bus do I take to City Hall?
   S2: Take the #11 bus.

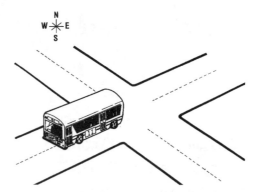

2. S1: Does Bus #1 go to City Hall?
   S2: No, it goes west to the beach.

3. S1: Where does she get on the bus?
   S2: She gets on at Western.

4. S1: Is he getting off the bus now?
   S2: Yes, he is.

★ Something Extra: Transfers

Maria wants to go shopping at a department store downtown, but bus #45 does not go downtown. Maria changes from Bus #45 to Bus #22 on Broadway. She needs a transfer.

☛ Practice: "Transfer to the #45 bus"

1. S1: Does this bus go to Vernon and King?
   S2: No, it doesn't.
   S1: Transfer to the #45 bus on Beverly.

2. S1: Does this bus go downtown?
   S2: No, it doesn't.
   S1: Change to the #22 bus on Broadway.

☛ Practice Activity: A map of the school

1. In a group, draw a map of the streets and the bus lines around your school.
2. One judge from each group look at all the maps and choose the best map.
3. Draw the winning map on the board.

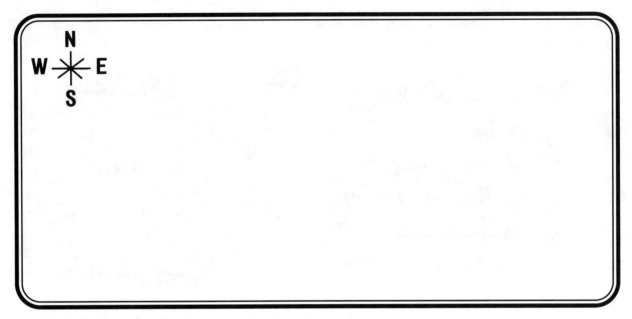

★ Something Extra: Go/Go to/Go to the

Go	Go to	Go to the
east/west	school	market
north/south	work	park
downtown	class	museum
home	bed	bedroom

1. Where do you go every day?   I _____ work.

2. Where do you go after work?   I _____.

3. Where does she go to buy clothes?   She _____.

4. Where do they go to buy groceries?   They _____.

5. Where are you going now?   We're _____ a party.

Reading: Does This Bus Go Downtown?

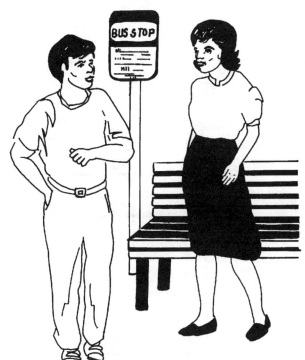

Ruben: Does this bus go downtown?

Mrs. Olmos: No, it doesn't. Where do you want to go?

Ruben: I want to go to the Grand Central Market.

Mrs. Olmos: Get off on Broadway and transfer to the #22 bus going north. Then get off on 3rd Street.

Ruben: How much is the fare?

Mrs. Olmos: It's 90 cents and 10 cents for the transfer.

Discussion

1. Where does Ruben want to go?
2. Where is the Grand Central Market?
3. What bus goes to the market?
4. Why does Ruben need a transfer?
5. How much is the bus fare?
6. Does your city have a good bus system?

✎ Writing

Look at page 179 and fill in the blanks.

1. Central Adult School is at the corner of _____ and _____.

2. Take the #6 bus going _____ on _____.

3. Take the #11 bus going _____ on _____.

4. Does the #14 bus go to the school? _____.

A. Listen and mark the direction with an arrow.

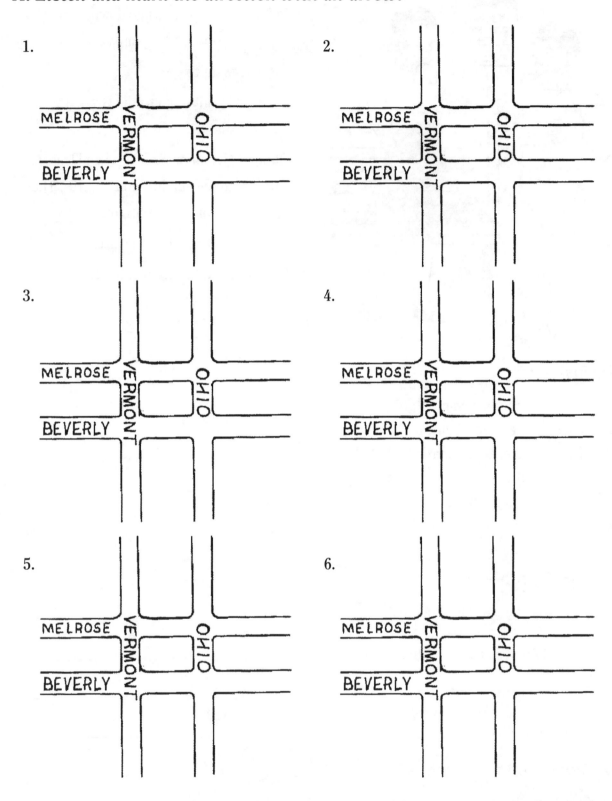

1.

2.

3.

4.

5.

6.

B. Read the bus routes and look at the map.

Read the questions and circle the answers.

1. The #4 bus goes west on Madison and turns right on Lincoln. It goes north on Lincoln.

   Does the #4 bus go to the post office?

   YES   NO

2. The #9 bus goes north on Lincoln and makes a left on Madison. It goes west to Jackson.

   Does the #9 bus go to the library?

   YES   NO

3. The #19 bus goes east on Washington to Lincoln, turns right on Lincoln and goes south to Jefferson. It turns left on Jefferson and continues east.

   Does the #19 bus go to the mall?

   YES   NO

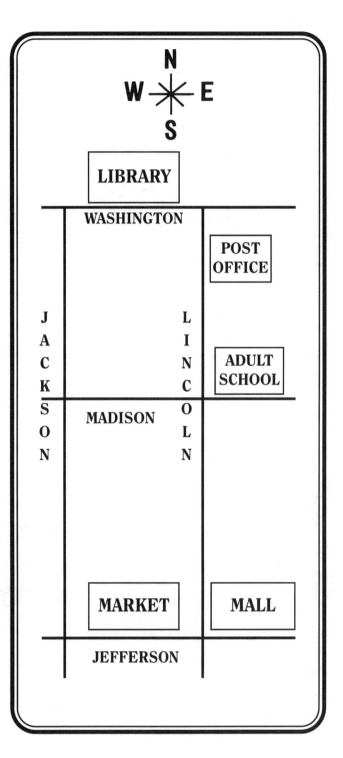

C. *Just for fun: Create a bus route.*

Tell the bus route from the mall to the library. Draw the route below.

Notes

Lesson 44

How Do You Go to Work?

Objectives: In this lesson you will learn to talk about getting around in a small town or a big city.

✔ Review: Does This Bus Go to the Market?

1. Draw two lines on the chalkboard and label them north, south, east, west.
2. Name the east–west street for a street in your city and draw Bus #1 on the line.
3. Name the north–south street for a street in your city and draw Bus #2 on the line.
4. Draw a market at the corner of the two streets.
5. Ask and answer questions about the two bus lines.

Something New: She Takes the Bus to Work
Listen and Look

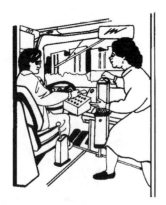
She takes the bus to work.

He drives to work.

He carpools.

They take the subway to work.

They walk to work.

☞ Practice Activity: How do you come to school?

How do you go to work? How do you come to school?

I take the bus.
I come by bus.

I drive.
I come by car.

I walk.
I come on foot.

Let's Talk: I Come by Bus

Sonia: Where do you live, Jae?

Jae: I live on Adams Street near Vermont. It's about two miles from here.

Sonia: How do you come to work?

Jae: I come by bus now. But I'm learning to drive.

☞ Practice: "I live on Madison near 9th"

1. S1: Where do you live?
   S2: I live on Madison near 9th.

2. S1: Where does Lila live?
   S2: She lives downtown.

3. S1: Does Bill live near you?
   S2: Yes, he does. He lives in the next block.

4. S1: How does your husband get to work?
   S2: He rides with a neighbor.

☞ Practice: "How far do you live from school?"

5. S1: How far do you live from school?
   S2: I live about a mile from here.

6. S1: How far does she live from school?
   S2: Not very far. Just a block away.

7. S1: Do your children live near school?
   S2: No, they don't.
   S1: How do they get to school?
   S2: They take the bus.

☛ Practice Activity: How far?

1. Talk about where you live and how far you live from school. See who lives close to school and who lives far from school.
2. Ask and answer the question, "How far do you live from school?"
3. Report to the class.

★ Something Extra: Names of Streets

Some streets are **avenues**:

Fifth Avenue

Park Ave.

Some streets are **streets**:

42nd Street

Basin St.

Some streets are **boulevards**:

Avalon Boulevard

Adams Blvd.

What are some other names for streets?

_____

_____

_____

_____

☛ Practice Activity: Take a poll

Take a poll of the students in class.

How many live on streets?   _____

on avenues?   _____

on boulevards?   _____

on others?   _____

Reading: Getting Around

Esteban lives in a big city. There are buses, subways, and elevated trains in his city. Esteban can get around the city easily.

Dinh lives in a small town. There is no local bus line or subway there. Dinh doesn't have a car. He gets around on a bicycle or on foot. Sometimes his friends give him a ride.

Discussion

1. How does Esteban get around in his city?
2. Do you think Esteban wants a car? Why?
3. How does Dinh get around his town?
4. Do you think Dinh wants a car?

✎ Writing

Write the questions and answers.

1. Where does Esteban live?

   _____ .

2. Are there buses and subways in a big city?

   _____ .

3. _____ ?

   He lives in a small town.

4. _____ ?

   He gets around on a bicycle or on foot.

5. _____ ?

   No, there isn't.

A. Listen and match the people to the way they get around.

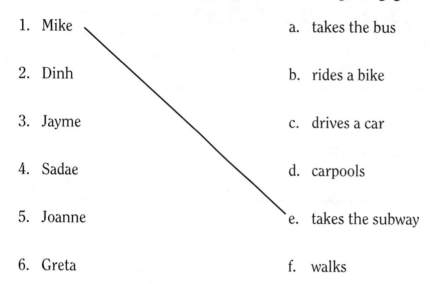

1. Mike   a. takes the bus

2. Dinh   b. rides a bike

3. Jayme   c. drives a car

4. Sadae   d. carpools

5. Joanne   e. takes the subway

6. Greta   f. walks

B. Group Grid: How do you get around?

Ask and answer these questions in your group of five.

    1. How do you come to school?

    2. How do you go to work?

    3. How do you go to the market?

Name	to school	to work	to the market
Roxanna	*by bus*	*by car*	*on foot*

C. Look at the box and complete the sentences.

bus	drives	far	goes
lives	near	school	works

Mila _____ five miles from _____. She _____ to

school every day. Her mother's office is _____ Mila's school and she takes Mila to

school in the morning. In the afternoon, Mila goes home by _____. Mila's father

_____ downtown. It's very _____ from their home and he

_____ to work.

D. Write your answers. Then ask your partner the questions.

	You	Your Partner
1. How do you come to school?		
2. How far do you live from school?		
3. Do you like to drive?		
4. Do you like to take the bus?		
5. Do you like to walk?		
6. Do you ride a bicycle?		
7. Do you like big cities or small towns?		
8. Do you come from a small town or a big city?		

We Danced All Night

Objectives: In this lesson you will learn to talk about past activities.

✔ Review: How Do You Come to School?

1. Ask the students in your group, "How do you come to school?"
2. Then tell the class about your group.

   Who walks to school?   Who carpools?

   Who drives to school?   Who gets a ride to school?

   Who comes by bus?

Something New: Mark's Day Off
Listen and Look

On his day off, Mark cleans his apartment, washes his clothes, plays soccer, and visits his girlfriend. Yesterday was his day off.

He cleaned his apartment.

He washed his clothes at the laundromat.

He played soccer at the park.

He visited his girlfriend.

☛ Practice: "What does Mark do on his day off?"

What does Mark do on his day off?	He cleans his apartment.
Does he vacuum the floor?	Yes, he does.
Does he mow the lawn?	No, he doesn't.
What did Mark do yesterday?	He dusted the furniture.
Did he mop the floor?	No, he didn't.
Did he wash his sheets?	Yes, he did.

Let's Talk: We Danced All Night

Rosa is buying vegetables from Mark.

Rosa: Hi, Mark. Did you enjoy your day off yesterday?

Mark: Yes, I did. I'm tired today.

Rosa: What did you do?

Mark: I played soccer all afternoon. Then Sue and I danced all night.

Rosa: All night?

Mark: Well, until 1:00 AM.

Discussion

1. Did Mark have a day off yesterday?
2. When did he play soccer?
3. How long did he and Sue dance?
4. How does Mark feel today?

☛ Practice: "I cleaned house all day"

1. S1: What did you do yesterday?
   S2: I cleaned house all day.

2. S1: What did she do last night?
   S2: She watched TV.

3. S1: Did you visit your friends yesterday?
   S2: Yes, I did.

4. S1: Did he play soccer all afternoon?
   S2: No, he didn't. He rested.

5. S1: What do you do on your day off?
   S2: We work in the yard.
   S1: Did you plant flowers yesterday?
   S2: No, we cleaned the yard.

6. S1: What does she do on her day off?
   S2: She cooks and bakes.
   S1: What did she bake yesterday?
   S2: She baked a cake.

■ Interaction: My Day Off

Walk around the room and ask questions. Write the answers in the spaces below.

Examples: What do you do on your day off every week?
            What did you do on your day off this week?

Name	Day off	Do every week	Did on day off
Kim	*Monday*	*visit friends*	*watched TV*

Reading: A Family Evening

Tomas Gomez likes to watch TV. He watched a baseball game last night. Then he watched the 11:00 o'clock news. He enjoys sports and the news.

Sara Gomez, his wife, didn't want to watch the game, so she hemmed a skirt for her daughter Lisa and listened to the radio.

Lisa and her brother Tom studied for an hour, then watched the baseball game with their father.

Discussion

1. What programs does Tomas enjoy?
2. What did he watch last night?
3. Sara didn't watch TV. Why?
4. What did Sara do?

5. Did Lisa and Tom watch the game all evening? What did they do first?
6. What kind of TV programs do you enjoy?

✍ Writing

Think about Mark's day off activities from pages 196–197 and answer the questions.

1. What does Mark usually do on his day off?

   _____

   _____

2. What did he do on his day off this week?

   _____

   _____

3. What did you do on your last day off? Write about it.

   _____

   _____

   _____

   _____

   _____

   _____

   _____

   _____

A. *What did he do on his day off?*

Partner 1 look at this page. Partner 2 look at page 202.

Ask and answer questions about the missing information.

Ask the questions: What does _____ usually do on Saturday?

What did _____ do last Saturday?

Partner 1

Who?	Usually	Last Saturday
Ted	watches TV	
Alice		watched a video
Bob	mows the lawn	
Carol	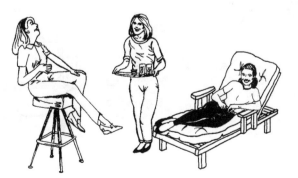	stayed home

Partner 2 look at this page. Partner 1 look at page 201.

Ask and answer questions about the missing information.

Ask the questions: What does _____ usually do on Saturday?

                             What did _____ do last Saturday?

Partner 2

Who?	Usually	Last Saturday
Ted		played soccer
Alice	cleans the house	
Bob		danced until 1:00 AM
Carol	visits friends	

B. Tic Tac Toe: Pick a square and answer the question.

Play Tic Tac Toe with five students.

Two people are the **X** team and two people are the **O** team. One student is the referee. The referee asks the questions and the teams answer the questions.

Notes

Unit Fifteen | Evaluation

I. Listening Comprehension

Listen and circle the correct answer, A or B.

1.

A   B

2.

A   B

3.

A   B

4.

A   B

5.

A. Yes, I did.   B. Yes, he does.

6.

A. Yes, they did.   B. Yes, they do.

II. Reading

Circle the correct answers.

1. He goes to school by bus. He
   _____ the bus at Main and Western.

   get on   gets on   drives

2. He _____ the bus at Main
   and Wilton.

   get off   takes   gets off

3. He _____ a transfer.

   need   doesn't need   doesn't needs

4. The bus _____ east on Main.

   go   going   goes

III. Writing

Write the correct words in the blanks.

1. What _____ Bill _____
   yesterday?

2. He _____ friends.

3. _____ he _____ soccer in the afternoon?

4. Yes, he _____.

5. _____ Sara _____ a baseball
   game last night?

6. _____, she _____.

7. _____ did she _____?

8. She _____ a dress for Lisa.

206

Delta's Apple Pie, Book 1B

Unit Sixteen

Working Men and Women

I Worked in a Bank

Objectives: In this lesson you will learn to ask and answer questions about your work experience.

✔ **Review:** My Day Off

1. In a group, discuss your days off.

   Examples: When is your day off?

                     What do you do on your day off every week?

                     What did you do on your last day off?

2. Report to the class on your group's day–off activities.

Something New: What Did He Do in His Country?

Listen and Look

He worked in a bakery. He baked cakes.

She worked in an office. She typed letters.

He worked in a garage. He repaired trucks.

She worked in a department store.
She waited on customers.

He worked on a farm. He raised cows.

She worked in a factory. She sewed blouses.

☛ Practice: "He worked in a garage"

1. S1: Where did he work in his country?
   S2: He worked in a garage.

2. S1: Where did he work in his country?
   S2: He worked in a factory.

3. S1: Where did she work in her country?
   S2: She worked in an office.
   S1: What did she do?
   S2: She typed letters.

4. S1: Where did he work in his country?
   S2: He worked in a body shop.
   S1: What did he do?
   S2: He painted cars.

Let's Talk: I Worked in a Bank

Mario is visiting Alicia at her home.

Alicia: Papa, this is Mario, a friend from Ecuador.

Mr. Rubio: Hello, Mario. Do you work with Alicia?

Mario: No, I don't. I'm attending a computer school.

Mr. Rubio: What did you do in your country?

Mario: I worked in a bank, but I didn't learn to use computers.

☛ **Practice: "He's attending computer school"**

MOVIE RENTAL

1. S1: Where did Mario work in his country?
   S2: He worked in a bank.
   S1: What is he doing now?
   S2: He's attending a computer school.

2. S1: What did Elena do in her country?
   S2: She waited on customers in a department store.
   S1: What is she doing now?
   S2: She's working in a video store.

☛ **Practice: "Yes, she did"**

3. S1: Did Yoko work in a factory
       in her country?

   S2: Yes, she did.

   S1: Is she working in a factory now?

   S2: No, she isn't.

4. S1: Did Manny work on a farm
       in his country?

   S2: Yes, he did.

   S1: Is he working on a farm now?

   S2: No, he isn't.

5. S1: Did Rita attend business school
       in her country?

   S2: No, she didn't.

   S1: What did she do?

   S2: She worked in an office.

6. S1: Did Kim work in a bank
       in his country?

   S2: No, he didn't.

   S1: What did he do?

   S2: He attended school.

■ Interaction: What Are You Doing Now?

1. In a group discuss these questions:

   Where are you from?

   What did you do in your country?

   What are you doing now?

2. Make a new group and continue the same conversation.

★ Something Extra: Pronunciation

/–t/	/–d/	/ɪd/
typed	**sewed**	**painted**
worked	listened	visited
touched	played	needed
crossed	repaired	wanted

She typed a letter.
They crossed the street.

She sewed a blouse.
He listened to the teacher.

He painted cars.
We visited our children.

1. Listen to the teacher.

Hold up 1 finger when you hear the /–t/ sound at the end of the word.
Hold up 2 fingers when you hear the /–d/ sound at the end of the word.
Hold up 3 fingers when you hear the /ɪd/ sound at the end of the word.

2. Say the following sentences in the past tense.

Examples: He works in a bank.   He worked in a bank.
            He's slowing down.   He slowed down.

a. She listens to her mother.
b. They stop at the signal.
c. He wants a hot dog.
d. He's painting his house.
e. We need a new book.
f. She's walking home.
g. He repairs cars.
h. She's starting the car.

Reading: Graciela Needs a License

Graciela owned a beauty shop in her country. Now Graciela is working at May's Beauty Shop. She is a shampoo person. She wants to work as a hairdresser in the United States, but she does not have a license. First she needs to learn English. Then she can take the test for a beauty operator license.

Discussion

1. Where did Graciela work in her country?
2. What is she doing now?
3. Why can't she work as a hairdresser now?
4. What does she need to do?

✍ Writing

Write 3–4 sentences about yourself.

1. What I did in my country:

_____

_____

_____

_____

2. What I am doing now:

_____

_____

_____

_____

A. Listen and match the name with the occupation.

1. Carlos   _____   a. baker

2. Sue   _____   b. seamstress

3. Yasu   _____   c. salesclerk

4. Carla   _____   d. mechanic

5. Lionel   _____   e. secretary

6. Paula   _____   f. farmer

B. Answer the questions about the people above.

1. Did Paula sew skirts? _____

2. Did Lionel repair cars or motorcycles? _____

3. Where did Carla work? _____

4. Did Sue work in a department store? _____

5. Where did Carlos work? _____

6. Where did Yasu work? _____

C. Walk around the room and ask about work experience.

Ask and answer the question: *Where did you work in your country?*
Make an **X** under the correct answer for each person.
Report your results to the class.

Name	Where did you work in your country?							
	Bakery	Garage	Office	Bank	Store	Factory	Farm	Other

Lesson 47

What Can You Do?

Objectives: In this lesson you will talk about things that people are able to do.

✔ Review: What Did You Do in Your Country?

1. Discuss your past and present jobs.

   Examples: What did you do in your country?

   Where did you work?

   What are you doing now?

2. Write the information on the board.

What I did	Where I worked	What I am doing now
sewed dresses	in a factory	studying English

Something New: People and Their Work
Listen and Look

He's an auto mechanic.   She's a seamstress.   She's a bus driver.

He can repair cars.   She can sew dresses.   She can drive a bus.

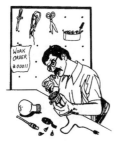

He's an electrician.   He's a plumber.   She's a hairdresser.
He can fix the lights.   He can repair pipes.   She can cut hair.

☛ Practice: "He's an electrician"

1. S1: What's his occupation?   2. S1: What's her occupation?
   S2: He's an electrician.   S2: She's a seamstress.

☛ Practice: "He can fix pipes"

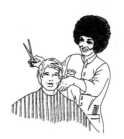

3. S1: What can a plumber do?   4. S1: What can she do?
   S2: He can fix pipes.   S2: She can cut hair.

☛ Practice: "What can he do?"

5. S1: What's his occupation?   6. S1: What's her occupation?
   S2: He's an auto mechanic.   S2: She's a bus driver.
   S1: What can he do?   S1: What can she do?
   S2: He - - - - - - - - - - .   S2: She - - - - - - - - - - .

Let's Talk: We Have a Flat Tire

Elsa Soto took Roberto and his friend to the park. Now they are getting ready to go home.

Elsa:	Oh, no. We have a flat tire.
Roberto:	Let's call Papa!
Elsa:	No, I can change the tire.
Roberto:	Are you sure, Mama?
Elsa:	Of course I can. Let's get the spare tire and the tools out of the trunk.

☞ Practice: "Yes, she can"

1. S1: Can she drive?
    S2: Yes, she can.

2. S1: Can he change a tire?
    S2: Yes, he can.

3. S1: Can he fix pipes?
    S2: No, he can't.
    S1: What can he do?
    S2: He can fix the lights.

4. S1: Can she bake a cake?
    S2: No, she can't.
    S1: What can she do?
    S2: She can make a shirt.

★ Something Extra: More People and Their Work
Listen and Look

She's a nurse's aide.
She can take temperatures.

He's a florist.
He can arrange flowers.

He's a short–order cook.
He can make hamburgers.

She's an artist.
She can paint pictures.

☛ Practice Activity: What else can they do?

Talk about the things the people in these and other occupations can do.

Occupation	What they can do
Auto mechanic	*repair motors, change tires, etc.*
Nurse's aide	
Florist	
Fast–food cook	

Other Occupations	What they can do
_____	_____
_____	_____
_____	_____
_____	_____
_____	_____

Reading: The Homemaker

A homemaker takes care of the house and family. Sometimes a homemaker is a woman. But these days, a homemaker is sometimes a man.

A homemaker starts work early in the morning and finishes late at night. He or she cleans, cooks, washes, gardens, shops, and takes care of the children. Then homemakers look after their spouses.

Discussion

1. Do you think homemaking is an important occupation?
2. Does a homemaker earn a good salary?
3. Are you a homemaker? If you are, tell about your daily activities.

✍ Writing

The reading on page 220 described the daily activities of a homemaker. Rewrite the story, telling about the homemaker's activities yesterday.

Yesterday, she started her work _____

_____

_____

_____

_____

_____

_____

_____

_____

_____

_____

A. Listen and circle the correct picture.

1.

    a.   b.   c.

2.

    a.   b.   c.

3.

    a.   b.   c.

4.

    a.   b.   c.

5.

    a.   b.   c.

B. Read and answer the questions. Then ask your partner.

	You	Your Partner
1. Can you speak English?	_____	_____
2. Can you repair cars?	_____	_____
3. Can you cook?	_____	_____
4. Can you sew?	_____	_____
5. Can you play a guitar?	_____	_____
6. Can you drive a truck?	_____	_____
7. Can you change a tire?	_____	_____
8. Can you cut hair?	_____	_____
9. Can you type?	_____	_____
10. Can you fix things?	_____	_____

C. BINGO!!

Ask and answer "Can you _____?" questions. Get a signature when the answer is yes. Get five signatures in a row and you can shout BINGO!!

"Can you _____*?"*				
play the guitar _____	speak Spanish _____	speak Chinese _____	speak English _____	make a cake _____
repair cars _____	type _____	take shorthand _____	play the piano _____	sew _____
cut hair _____	change a tire _____	drive a car _____	ride a bicycle _____	paint _____
dance _____	drive a truck _____	cook _____	bake _____	arrange flowers _____
stand on one foot _____	pronounce my name _____	play soccer _____	say the alphabet _____	sing a song _____

D. Talk about the pictures.

Jack Ho is looking for a job. He's talking to Ms. Green in her office.

1.

2.

3.

4.

5.

6.

E. Write the questions from the dialogue.

1. _How are you today, Mr. Ho?_____
2. _____
3. _____
4. _____
5. _____
6. _____

F. Act out the interview with your partner.

I Can't Take Shorthand

Objectives: In this lesson you will learn to talk about things that people can and cannot do.

✔ Review: Occupations

What can people in these occupations do?

auto mechanic	seamstress	carpenter	nurse's aide
hairdresser	electrician	homemaker	plumber

Something New: What I Can't Do
Listen and Look

I can sing,
but I can't dance.

He can read English,
but he can't speak it.

He can cook,
but he can't bake.

She can type, but she can't
take shorthand.

He can stand,
but he can't walk.

☞ Practice: "Yes, I can" or "No, I can't"

1. S1: Can you dance?
   S2: Yes, I can.

2. S1: Can you sing?
   S2: No, I can't.

3. S1: Can the baby crawl?
   S2: Yes, he can.
   S1: Can he walk?
   S2: No, he can't.

4. S1: Can Maria drive?
   S2: Yes, she can.
   S1: Can she drive on the freeway?
   S2: No, she can't.

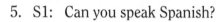

5. S1: Can you speak Spanish?
   S2: I can speak Spanish,
      but I can't write it.

6. S1: Can your husband cook?
   S2: He can make breakfast,
      but he can't make dinner.

Let's Talk: I Can't Take Shorthand

Mona is applying for a job as a secretary.

Manager: Can you type?
Mona: Yes, I can, but I can't take shorthand.
Manager: Can you use the computer?
Mona: No, I can't, but I can learn.
Manager: All right. You can start as a general office clerk.

★ Something Extra: Pronunciation

Practice saying the dark words louder and stronger.

Note: The word *can* is pronounced very fast and is not strong.

"can"	"can't"
I can **type**.	I **can't** take shorthand.
I can **sing**.	I **can't** dance.
He can **paint**.	He **can't** draw.
She can **drive** a bus.	She **can't** drive a truck.
My son can **crawl**.	He **can't** walk yet.
They can **fix** cars.	They **can't** fix computers.

Reading: A Musician's Life

Luis played in a mariachi band in his country. His band worked in a restaurant. Luis can play the guitar and the violin. He can also sing.

Luis wanted to work as a full–time musician in this country, but he can't earn enough money. So he works in a print shop five days a week.

Luis and his mariachi band play at Lupe's Restaurant on Saturday and Sunday nights.

Discussion

1. What is Luis doing for a living?
2. What would Luis like to do?
3. What did Luis do in his country?
4. Where did he work?
5. What can Luis do?
6. What does Luis do on weekends?
7. Do you think he's happy?

✍ Writing

Ask or answer the questions.

1. Where _____ Luis _____ in his country? He _____ in a restaurant.

2. Where _____ he _____ now? He is _____ in a print shop.

3. _____ Luis sing? Yes, he _____.

4. What _____ Luis want to do? He _____ to work as a musician.

☛ Practice Activity

1. Make a list of things that you:

can do	can't do	want to do
_____	_____	_____
_____	_____	_____
_____	_____	_____
_____	_____	_____
_____	_____	_____
_____	_____	_____
_____	_____	_____
_____	_____	_____

2. Make a group and talk about your lists.

Lesson 48 Activity Pages

A. Listen to the people. Circle can or can't.

1. Martha   (can) / can't   cook.

2. Jim   can / can't   cook.

3. Will   can / can't   speak Spanish.

4. Roger   can / can't   repair cars.

5. Susan   can / can't   drive a car.

6. Jung   can / can't   type.

B. Talk about the chart.

✔ = can ✘ = can't							
	type	use a computer	answer phones	cook	bake	repair a car	change a tire
Norma	✘	✘	✔	✔	✔	✘	✔
Fred	✘	✘	✔	✘	✘	✘	✔
Rheta	✔	✔	✔	✘	✘	✘	✘
Robert	✔	✘	✔	✔	✘	✔	✔
Renee	✔	✔	✔	✔	✔	✘	✔

C. Use the information from the chart to write sentences.

1. *Norma can answer phones, but she can't type.*

2. _____

3. _____

4. _____

5. _____

6. _____

D. Ask three students about what they can do.

	✔ = can		X = can't				
Name	type	use a computer?	answer phones?	cook?	bake?	repair a car?	change a tire?

E. Use the information in exercise D to write sentences.

1. _____

2. _____

3. _____

Unit Sixteen

I. Listening Comprehension

Listen and circle the correct answer, A or B.

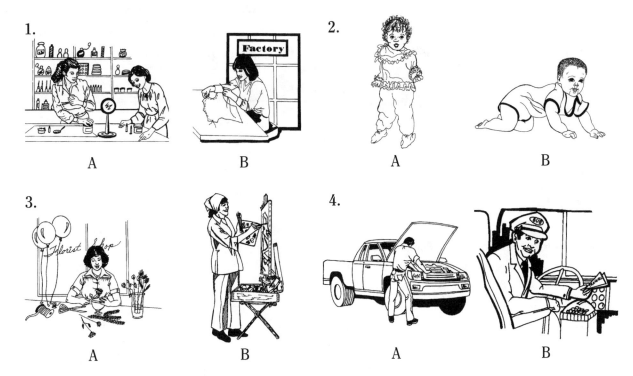

1.

A   B

2.

A   B

3.

A   B

4.

A   B

5.

A. Yes, she can.
B. Yes, she did.

6.

A. No, she isn't.
B. No, she doesn't.

II. Reading

Circle the correct answers.

1. Where did Ben _____ in his country?

    work   works   worked

2. _____ you type?

    Are   Can   Does

3. Is she _____ a cake?

    bakes   baked   baking

4. Can she drive a bus?

    _____

    Yes, she did.
    Yes, she does.
    Yes, she can.

III. Writing

Choose the correct word for each sentence.

1. He's an _____.

    He _____ in a garage.

    He can _____ cars.

2. What's his _____?

    He's an _____.

    _____ he fix the lights?

    Yes, he can.

3. What _____ she do in her country?

    She worked in an _____.

    Did she _____ shorthand?

    No, she _____.

auto mechanic
Can
can't
did
didn't
does
electrician
fix
occupation
office
repair
take
works

Notes

Notes